Buyer Agency Today

4th Edition

Keeping Your Competitive Edge in Real Estate

GAIL LYONS and **DON HARLAN**

Dearborn™
Real Estate Education

This publication is designed to provide accurate and authoritative information in regard to the subject matter covered. It is sold with the understanding that the publisher is not engaged in rendering legal, accounting, or other professional service. If legal advice or other expert assistance is required, the services of a competent professional person should be sought.

President: Roy Lipner
Vice-President of Product Development and Publishing: Evan Butterfield
Associate Publisher: Louise Benzer
Senior Development Editor: Tony Peregrin
Director of Production: Daniel Frey
Quality Assurance Editor: David Shaw
Typesetting: Maria Warren
Creative Director: Lucy Jenkins

© 1979, 1980, 1985, 1990, 1996, 2005 by Dearborn™ Real Estate Education, a division of Dearborn Financial Publishing, Inc.®

Published by Dearborn™ Real Estate Education, a division of Dearborn Financial Publishing, Inc.®
30 South Wacker Drive, Suite 2500
Chicago, IL 60606-7481
(312) 836-4400
http://www.dearbornRE.com

Printed in the United States of America.

05   06   07   10   9   8   7   6   5   4   3   2   1

Contents

About the Authors

Gail G. Lyons, ABR, CRS, CIPS, CCIM, CRB, SRES, DREI, QSC, C-REC, is broker/owner of Boulder Real Estate Services, Ltd. in Boulder, Colorado, a business she founded in 1985. Licensed since 1973, Gail is an active practitioner who represents both buyers and sellers. During her career, she has been president of her local association—the Colorado Association of REALTORS®—and has held numerous leadership roles within the National Association of REALTORS®. Her current position is Regional Coordinator for the Asia-Pacific Region.

As an author and global instructor, Gail has used her broad experience as a foundation for numerous articles and five books in addition to *Buyer Agency Today: Keeping Your Competitive Edge in Real Estate.* These include *Consensual Dual Agency: A Practical Approach to the In-House Sale* and *The Future of Real Estate,* which are coauthored with her partner in Harlan Lyons & Associates, Don Harlan.

Gail has won awards from her peers including REALTOR® of the Year from both her local association and the Colorado Association of REALTORS®. In addition, she is a member of NAR's Real Estate Buyer Agent's Council (REBAC) Hall of Fame.

She lives in Longmont, Colorado, with her husband, Harley, and Abyssinian cat, Ramsses, on their 20-acre eco-farm.

Don Harlan, CCIM, CRE, ABR, DREI, CRB, GRI, CIPS, C-CREC, has been an active REALTOR® for 32 years in both commercial and residential real estate as well as an author, teacher, trainer, and consultant. He has managed several companies and has presented seminars and courses all over the United States and Canada, as well as Eastern Europe.

Don has been very involved in teaching ethics and is the coauthor of *Real Estate Ethics: Good Ethics = Good Business* with William H. Pivar. He has also served as president of both the Denver Board of REALTORS® as well as the Colorado Association of REALTORS®, and he was named the REALTOR® of the Year for both organizations.

Don and his wife, Kay, live in Denver, Colorado, close to two of their five children and all of their six grandchildren.

The Harlan-Lyons team wrote the first three editions of *Buyer Agency,* and they have collaborated once again on the new edition—*Buyer Agency Today: Keeping Your Competitive Edge in Real Estate.* They are credited with establishing this buyer/ agency relationship as the accepted and standard practice utilized today.

Acknowledgments

No book can be written without the assistance and advice of colleagues—many of whom are also authors. Several of these you will find quoted throughout the book and to them we say "thanks"—your experience has made this book come alive.

However, we owe a very special thanks to four educators from the Real Estate Educators Association who agreed to act as critics, editors, and reviewers. Each read the third edition and offered suggestions as to changes and modifications each felt necessary to make this new edition contemporaneous. We combined their input with our own experience and research, making revisions and writing new material. Our final draft was again reviewed by these four and more tweaking was done. We hope the final result that you hold in your hands will lead you to higher income and greater professionalism. If it does, it could not have been done without the input and honest criticism of Marcie Roggow, DREI; Tim Meline, DREI;

Roger Turcotte, DREI; and Marie Spodek, DREI. We are indeed proud and honored to call you all friends as well as colleagues.

Of course, we also owe great thanks to our spouses, Kay and Harley, who put up with our early and late hours at the computer, our bouts of frustration, and our times of joy.

Finally, we'd like to acknowledge and thank Dearborn Publishing, and in particular, Tony Peregrin, Senior Development Editor.

Preface

*B*uyer Agency Today: Keeping Your Competitive Edge in Real Estate is a major revision of *Buyer Agency: Your Competitive Edge in Real Estate,* which was initially published in 1990 and has had three editions. Hailed by many critics as the leading text on the subject of buyer representation, this new version is designed to assist current practitioners in honing their skills to reach the next level of professionalism.

Highlights of the many changes include a thorough discussion of many niche markets that can be developed by today's buyer's agent into successful profit centers as well as a useful and expanded appendix section that includes examples of key forms and contracts. The text has been thoroughly revised to accurately reflect today's market environment and conditions.

We hope you enjoy this book and that you find it a useful reference in your daily practice.

A Revolution…in Hindsight

From the perspective of the first decade of the 21st century, buyer agency has rapidly grown from an unregulated practice used by a small minority in the mid-1980s to *the* way to do business today, a highly regulated way. A brief review of this revolution, its milestones, and environmental pressures, will provide useful background for readers who want to understand how buyer agency has become standard operating procedure before they begin studying today's legal and regulatory aspects as well as the important "how-tos" of representing buyer clients.

HISTORY OF BUYER AGENCY

Buyer agency traces its roots back to subagency, a legal doctrine that was developed by legal counsel of the National Association of REALTORS® (NAR) to prevent any nonmembers (either for-sale-by-owners or nonmember licensees) of multiple-listing services (MLS) from being able to enter information about their property listings in the MLS catalog. Under this theory, all members of the MLS *represented the seller* whether they were listing or selling agents, and therefore, the information contained in the MLS could be treated as proprietary. The MLS was thus not a marketing device but a method by which members of the service could share information about their clients' properties. Selling agents worked "with" buyers but did not represent them, because they were already the sellers' agents or subagents. The MLS as a "blanket unilateral offer of subagency" became NAR policy in the early 1970s.

Legal theory, however, and practice were often different as was shown by the historic 1984 Federal Trade Commission (FTC) study. Based on questions asked of California buyers and sellers, the study found the following:

- Of the buyers who worked with a cooperating agent (subagent) 71 percent felt that agent *represented* them.
- Of the buyers who worked with the listing agent, 31 percent felt that agent *represented* them.
- Overall, 57 percent of the buyers questioned believed that the agent they worked with *represented* them.
- Of the sellers questioned, 74 percent thought that the selling agent *represented* the buyers.

The reason for this misunderstanding on behalf of the public was, unfortunately, clear. A 1983 FTC study identified "non-disclosure of the broker's position (agency)" as a major problem for buyers. A 1987 Virginia study quantified this problem, finding that 55 percent of the buyers questioned claimed that the sales agent had failed to inform them that the agent represented the *seller*. In other words, agents legally represented sellers but behaved as though they represented buyers: this was *undisclosed dual agency*.

Insufficient education and training of real estate sales agents, combined with a natural desire to be helpful and a fear of the expected chilling effect agency disclosure might have, easily explain the confusion and misunderstanding among not only the public but also the agents who served them.

During the early to mid-1980s, a few real estate professionals began to seriously question why sellers should be the *only* parties represented in transactions. Barry Miller of Denver and others, including the authors, began teaching how to legally represent buyers by *rejecting* the MLS's blanket offer of subagency and providing client level services to buyers. In 1982, Miller founded an organization, the Real Estate Buyer Agents Council (REBAC), to provide support to these fledgling buyer agents.

These beginnings caught the attention of the NAR. William D. North, its chief legal counsel, stated in his 1986 *Agency White Paper:* "The issue is one of assuring that the consumer of real estate services is in a position to make knowledgeable, informed choices of whom he wants to represent him, if anyone; of the services he desires to receive; the liabilities he is prepared to accept; and the compensation he is willing to pay."

For consumers, making "knowledgeable, informed choices" required their knowing who their agents represented as well as the duties representation required. This meant agency disclosure. State regulatory bodies, feeling the pressure of both industry and consumer groups, began to develop legislation requiring such disclosure. Such legislation was first proposed at the state level in Massachusetts in 1977. A few states, of which Colorado was the notable example in 1984, further required that any agent who decided to be a buyer's agent must have the terms of the agency agreement in writing. Other states followed during the next decade although most required only written disclosure.

In March 1987, the federal government, through the Bureau of Consumer Protection of the Federal Trade Commission, issued a free brochure entitled *Facts for Consumers*. It framed the issue clearly, stating

> Any broker may agree to represent you, as the homebuyer, and some brokers are beginning to specialize in legally representing buyers. Having a "buyer's broker" may offer you some advantages. For example, a buyer's broker may be more motivated to spot problems with a home you are considering and may be able to obtain more favorable purchasing terms. Buyers' brokers may or may not charge you a fee. This is because a buyer's broker can legally share in the commission paid by the seller, as long as you (the homebuyer), the home seller, and the seller's broker agree to this. You can try to locate buyers' brokers by asking friends and looking for advertisements in your newspaper and the yellow pages.

By November 1988, the NAR board of directors further opened the traditional real estate market to buyers' agents by allowing its local associations "to utilize the MLS to also offer compensation to buyer agents, provided that a blanket, unilateral offer of subagency is made with respect to each listing submitted to the MLS."

In 1991/1992, NAR followed suit as its president, Harley E. Rhouda, appointed a Presidential Advisory Group (PAG) to study the current status of the industry relative to agency. The PAG's resultant report capsulated the changes deemed necessary to avoid undisclosed dual agency and encourage all possible types of agency while assuring that the public was aware of its options. The advisory group's recommendations included:

- NAR's multiple-listing policy should be modified to delete the *mandatory* offer of subagency and make all offers of subagency *optional*. Participants submitting listings to the MLS must, however, offer *cooperation* to other participants in the form of subagency or cooperation with *buyer agents* or both. All offers of subagency or cooperation made through an MLS must include an offer of compensation.

- NAR should encourage state associations to achieve, through legislation or regulation, state-mandated agency disclosure requiring all licensees to provide *timely, meaningful, written disclosure* to consumers of *all* possible types of agency relationships (i.e., buyer agency, seller agency, disclosed dual agency) available under state law and the most significant implications of choosing one type over another. This disclosure would permit consumers to make informed choices.

- NAR should encourage real estate firms to have a *written company policy* addressing agency relationships.

- NAR should emphasize the importance of education and training for all real estate licensees on the topic of agency and implement programs to accomplish this goal. State regulatory bodies that required prelicensing courses and core continuing education programs for licensees were encouraged to make agency programs part of those education requirements.

In general, the PAG's recommendations were implemented by resultant NAR policy as can be seen in this 1992 addition to the NAR Statement of Policy:

> The National Association of REALTORS® recognizes seller agency, buyer agency, and disclosed dual agency with informed consent as appropriate forms of consumer representation in real estate transactions. The association respects the need for all REALTORS® to be able to make individual business decisions about their companies' agency practices. Furthermore, NAR endorses freedom of choice and informed consent for consumers of real estate services when creating agency relationships with real estate licensees.

In April 1992, MLS policy was changed from a "blanket unilateral offer of *subagency*" to a "blanket unilateral offer of *cooperation.*" At almost the same time (November 1992), NAR's Code of Ethics was substantially amended to include articles directly related to various aspects of seller, buyer, and dual agency. Buyer agency had come of age!

By July 1, 1993, all REALTOR®-owned MLSs showed compensation to both subagents and buyers' agents, as the concept of "subagency optional" required that any offer of cooperation be tied to compensation. This allowed listing agents to offer cooperation/compensation to subagents, buyers' agents, or both. Many firms elected to no longer make the offer to subagents because of the perceived liability created for themselves and their sellers. This change resulted in an increase in buyer agency from less than 25 percent of the market to something in excess of 95 percent today.

Almost all states have now instituted agency disclosure legislation and/or regulation. Some have created new forms of brokerage relationships such as *transaction brokerage* to deal with the issue of buyers who did not want to be represented when agents no longer had the option of subagency and *designated agency* as an addition and/or alternative to disclosed dual agency. Nationwide the practice of subagency has disappeared because of market pressures and, occasionally, legislation.

During these early years of buyer agency, all, however, was not easy. It was not uncommon for listing agents and sellers to offer buyer agents cooperation but no or very little compensation relative to that offered subagents. Myths developed such as buyers' agents could not be paid by the seller, buyers will not pay for agency services, buyer agency is not recognized by lenders, and buyer agency makes buyers and sellers (and their agents) adversaries. All of these have been debunked and have proved to be just myths. Like most changes, buyer agency initially seemed uncomfortable to many even though it was just the other side of the agency coin. Seller agency and buyer agency were, and are, essentially identical in terms of fiduciary/statutory duties. In today's market, buyer agency has become standard operating procedure.

DISCLOSURE AND BUYER AGENCY

Because of its great importance to the growth of buyer agency, let's look at agency disclosure in greater detail. Agency disclosure, a regulatory/legislative requirement, began sweeping the nation in the mid-1980s. It is an ideal introduction to a discussion and offer of buyer representation but an often difficult undertaking for the traditional sellers' agents as well as nonagents.

For listing agents and nonagents who can't or don't want to offer buyer agency, this disclosure is uncomfortable and is still often done almost as an aside during preparation of the purchase agreement. Indeed, regulators of the real estate industry often point out that although disclosure is required, their evidence indicates that only a relatively small percentage of all agents are actually accomplishing disclosure at the first meaningful contact with a buyer. As a result of late and often ineffective disclosure, many buyers in turn become uneasy about their lack of representation and seek an alternative. It is thus not uncommon for a listing agent to receive an offer from a buyer's agent, who now represents the formerly uneasy buyer, to whom the listing agent had shown the property.

No matter how uncomfortable disclosure is, the seller's agent or nonagent is well advised to complete the disclosure to the buyer at the first practical moment. Disclosure should include not only the statement that the agent represents either the seller or no one but also a description of all the services a seller's agent or nonagent can provide to the buyer. It is also very important to remind the buyer not to disclose any confidential information to the seller's agent and/or nonagent—for example, the highest price he or she is willing to pay for the property—because it is the agent's duty to disclose that.

However, to be truly effective, the disclosure should also include the fact that the buyer who chooses to do so can be represented by an attorney, a buyer's agent, or both. Even without disclosure of their legal right to representation, buyers often learn about it through casual conversation, legal advice, or even the media. Then, some buyers elect to obtain representation after a seller's agent or a nonagent has spent a great deal of time working with them and may even have written an offer. At this point, the agents involved often get into a dispute over procuring cause (see Chapter 12).

As a result of the unease about lack of representation, many buyers begin searching for a buyer's agent, and disclosure can be said to have created a market for buyer agency. For buyers' agents, these same disclosure requirements provide an excellent way for them to begin a discussion and offer of representation, forcefully and clearly stating that the agent and his or her company have chosen to represent buyers (as well as sellers if that is the company policy). This is a perfect lead-in to the buyer counseling session described in Chapter 8.

Disclosure requirements are, therefore, welcomed by buyers' agents, as they help create an environment in which the agent's offer to represent the buyer is more likely to be accepted. Disclosure, however, is just the first step. To be successful, the buyer's agent must follow up with adequate and professional service that meets the buyer's needs and wants.

NAR's Policy on Agency Disclosure

The clearest description of the most effective agency disclosure was drafted by NAR in the late 1980s as the result of its PAG. These terms were generally incorporated into most state laws and/or regulations by the mid-1990s. The policy stated that all licensees should provide to consumers *timely, meaningful, and written disclosure of all possible types of brokerage relationships, and the most significant implications of choosing one type over another.*

The purpose of such timely, meaningful, and written disclosure was and is to permit consumers to make an informed choice.

Timely disclosure must take place before a representation agreement or contract is entered into. Disclosure to customers must take place before a licensee enters into *substantive* discussions about real estate needs and financial capabilities or exchanges any confidential information.

Meaningful disclosure must include all legal forms of brokerage relationships with consumers available under state law, even if the broker does not, as a matter of office policy, offer all of those options. For the buyer, this would include buyer agency, any statutory nonagency, and customer status, as well as a discussion of what relationships would result from an in-house sale (e.g., dual agency, designated brokerage).

Written disclosure refers to licensees' use of standard state disclosure forms. Such forms provide licensees with the assurance that their disclosure is adequate.

SUMMARY

Buyer agency began in the early to mid-1980s. During its early years, resistance was common. Its history in the 15 years between 1985 and 2000 was largely influenced by the acts of NAR, courts, and state regulatory bodies. The NAR policy on agency disclosure was especially formative. By the turn of the century, the market had thoroughly adopted buyer agency. Today, buyer agency is standard operating procedure in the minds of both real estate professionals and most consumers.

REVIEW QUESTIONS

1. Which is not a myth of buyer agency?
   a. Buyers' agents cannot use the MLS.
   b. Buyers' agents can be paid by the seller.
   c. Buyer agency is illegal.
   d. Buyers' agents' fees cannot be included in the sales price.

ANSWER:

b. Buyers' agents can be paid by anyone, including the seller, provided the source of the commission is disclosed. Items (a), (c), and (d) are untrue: buyers' agents can use the MLS, buyer agency is legal in every state, and buyers' agents' fees can be included in the sales price.

2. Initial agency disclosure should occur
   a. at the very first contact whether by phone, e-mail, letter, or in person.
   b. as soon as specific assistance is provided.
   c. at closing.
   d. in the offer to purchase.

ANSWER:

b. Agency disclosure must occur as soon as possible and in no case later than specific assistance is provided by the agent and confidential type information is discussed. To make disclosure at closing (c) or in the purchase offer (d) is too late. To make disclosure at the very first contact (a) is usually not practical.

CHAPTER | 2

Client Versus Customer and the Duties Owed to Each

In the recent past, owing to the long-standing tradition of subagency, most licensees were not legally considered the agents of buyers and, consequently, buyers technically were not represented. However, because many licensees during the late 1980s and early 1990s were unaware of agency relationships, they treated buyers as clients. Today, however, licensees are becoming fully knowledgeable and aware of what it means for the buyer to be a buyer client and, therefore, the principal.

DIFFERENCES BETWEEN CLIENTS AND CUSTOMERS

Let us for a moment put ourselves in the shoes of an unrepresented buyer customer. Do we really believe that he or she has any sense of being different from a buyer client? Certainly that perception of difference is unlikely if the buyer did not receive any counseling or disclosure. An exception would be a buyer who has had some exposure to consumer information such as either the Federal Trade Commission (FTC) or the Consumer Federation of America/AARP brochure or who has discussed the issue with knowledgeable friends or associates.

The buyer customer is entitled to fair and honest treatment but not to representation. The buyer client is entitled to full representation with all of the attendant responsibilities required by the agency relationship. As well-known author and agency pioneer James Warkentin said, "Fairness is not representation. Fairness means I'm not going to cheat you; representation means I'm going to take care of you." I will be your **advocate** and give you my advice regarding the purchase of any potential real estate.

The problem that occurred in the past is that most buyers thought they were going to be "taken care of," regardless of their agency status or relationship with their salesperson.

To clarify, let's define client and customer:

- Client—a buyer or seller who is represented by a salesperson or broker as the buyer's or seller's agent. Such agents are subject to that buyer's or seller's control. The terms of their agency agreement should be in writing and should define their fiduciary duties.
- Customer—usually a buyer who is working with a salesperson or broker who is the agent/subagent of the seller or who is a nonagent. It could also be a seller of an unlisted property who is working with a buyer's agent, although this situation is less common.

DUTIES AND RESPONSIBILITIES TO BUYER CLIENTS

The agency relationship requires that the agent adhere to fiduciary duties to the buyer. The most widely accepted list of fiduciary duties contains the following elements:

- Loyalty
- Disclosure
- Confidentiality
- Obedience
- Reasonable care and diligence in performance of the agency
- Accounting for all funds and documents under the agent's control

Loyalty

The agent must at all times be loyal to his or her principal. What is loyalty? *Webster's Ninth New Collegiate Dictionary* defines the word as "unswerving in allegiance or being faithful to a private person to whom fidelity is due." An amplification of this definition states that loyalty "implies a faithfulness that is steadfast in the face of any temptation to renounce, desert, or betray." A commonly used synonym for *loyalty* is the word *fidelity,* which is defined as "the quality or state of being faithful and implies strict and continuous faithfulness to an obligation, trust, or duty." These strong words should reinforce the seriousness of the requirement that you be loyal to your client.

Loyalty means that the interests of the principal come before and have absolute priority over the interests of the agent or any other person. The lure of a potential commission or fee must never interfere with your judgment of what is in the best interests of your client. This is one of the most common conflicts of interest that real estate salespeople face in their everyday business, particularly for newer licensees, who have not yet developed that sensitivity to potentially difficult situations. Because of their training, lawyers and accountants, on the other hand, are very sensitive to potential conflicts of interest. As real estate agents, we must develop similar habits and instincts.

Disclosure

This duty of loyalty also includes the honest and total disclosure of all facts and information that may affect the principal's decisions concerning the property or transaction. The agent is expected to know or be able to find out all of the pertinent information about any property or other aspect of the transaction that is the subject of the agency agreement. Real estate licensees today are expected to know about potential problems such as radon gas, expansive or peculiar soils, asbestos, hazardous waste, the need for property inspections, zoning problems, potential development in the vicinity, property taxes, community situations that might affect the use of the property by the buyer and much more.

As an agent, you may just throw up your hands and say, "How can I know everything? What are the limitations on what

I am expected to disclose?" Fortunately, there are general guidelines that do give some reasonable direction.

Disclosure Guidelines. Agents are not expected to know things that are outside the scope of their licensed authority or expertise. In other words, they are not expected to be engineers, contractors, architects, or lawyers. The key is to know when to say, "I don't know but I will find out," or "We had better talk to someone who is an expert on that who can give us reliable advice."

Article 2 of the NAR Code of Ethics states that:

REALTORS® shall avoid exaggeration, misrepresentation, or concealment of pertinent facts relating to the property or the transaction. REALTORS® shall not, however, be obligated to discover latent defects in the property, to advise on matters outside the scope of their real estate license, or to disclose facts which are confidential under the scope of agency duties owed to their clients. *(Amended 1/93)*

Standard of Practice 2–1 states that:

REALTORS® shall only be obligated to discover and disclose adverse factors reasonably apparent to someone with expertise in only those areas required by their real estate licensing authority. Article 2 does not impose upon the REALTOR® the obligation of expertise in other professional or technical disciplines. *(Amended 1/96)*

The general rule is that agents should know about the *physical aspects of the property* and should be able to rely on the owner of the property to disclose those facts to them. If disclosure of *personal information* about the seller or buyer might cause harm, a seller's or buyer's agent would not be expected to know or disclose it. Examples of such personal information include health, marital or family problems, financial difficulties, and similar matters. However, any such information can be disclosed only with the affected party's consent. If such disclosure would affect the other party's decision, the agent who is aware of such information may disclose it to the other party only with the client's consent.

However, confidential type information about the seller is sometimes available to the buyer's agent from public records, newspapers, gossip, and other nonconfidential sources. This information must be disclosed to the buyer client along with the source of the information.

There are six types of disclosures that should be explained to all potential buyers. Standard forms are generally available for the first two.

1. *Agency or brokerage relationship.* This disclosure is critical and definitely required at first contact or in the counseling session. In order to make an intelligent decision, the buyer consumer must understand the differences in the various relationships.
2. *Property disclosure prepared by the seller is for information to potential buyers.* This disclosure is one that requires the seller to disclose all known material defects of the property. This does not preclude the need for an independent professional inspection.

3. *Previous dealings.* Disclose and discuss any previous pertinent dealings or relationships with either the sellers or buyers to avoid any possible conflicts of interest.
4. *Possible conflicts of interest.* Clearly explain the possible conflicts of interest if the agent is buying the property personally or for a close friend, partner, or relative.
5. *Bonus offered by seller to the selling licensee*
6. *Properties that will not be shown by the buyer's agent* (i.e., unlisted properties and FSBOs)

Confidentiality

This fiduciary duty is a little trickier to deal with because there are many different perceptions of what is confidential. What is considered privileged information to one party may be of no concern whatever to another. Generally speaking, the only situations that can have some measure of protection on grounds of confidentiality are personal matters that the principal does not wish disclosed. Even if the principal requests confidentiality, the agent by law cannot refuse to disclose known material facts about the property.

If a buyer client discloses what he or she is willing to pay for a certain property, his or her agent must keep that confidential and not disclose it to the seller or the seller's listing agent. If a buyer customer discloses that same information, the selling agent who is the seller's agent/subagent *must* disclose it to the seller through the listing agent. Whether or not a nonagent must disclose such information depends on applicable state law.

The most unique aspect of this fiduciary duty is that confidentiality does not end with termination of the agency relationship itself; rather, the duty of confidentiality continues indefinitely. Article 1's Standard of Practice 1–9 provides further clarification:

> The obligation of REALTORS® to preserve confidential information provided by their clients continues after the termination of the agency relationship. REALTORS® shall not knowingly, during or following the termination of a professional relationship with their client:
>
> 1. reveal confidential information of the client; or
> 2. use confidential information of the client to the disadvantage of the client; or
> 3. use confidential information of the client for the REALTOR®'s advantage or the advantage of a third party unless the client consents after full disclosure except where:
>   a. the REALTOR® is required by court order; or
>   b. it is the intention of the client to commit a crime and the information is necessary to prevent the crime; or
>   c. it is necessary to defend the REALTOR® or the REALTOR®'s employees or associates against an accusation of wrongful conduct. (*Adopted 1/93, Amended 1/95*)

Obedience

The agent has the duty to obey the principal and to fulfill the requests of the client to the best of his or her ability. Any such request must generally conform to the purpose of the agency and, in the case of a buyer, the work that you are asked to perform will in almost all cases deal specifically with real estate and pertain to the transaction at hand.

The principal cannot, however, expect you to perform a task or exercise a duty that would cause you to break a law or violate a standard of care. One example of this exception would occur if the principal asked you to participate in an act of discrimination that would violate both civil rights laws and the National Association of REALTORS® Code of Ethics.

Reasonable Care and Diligence

This duty is really the essence of the assigned task according to the agreement between the principal and the agent. What exactly is reasonable care and diligence? This doctrine has changed considerably over the years, especially with the advent of buyer agency. Historically, the buyer under subagency was entitled to fair and honest treatment and disclosure of known facts. The subagent's role as a representative of the seller provided a fair amount of latitude in the showing of properties and preparation of contracts. However, the sole obligation of the buyer's agent is to the buyer, that is, to show properties without regard to seller relationships or listing considerations. Without question, the buyer client is entitled to expect a higher standard of performance than is the buyer customer.

The word *reasonable* deserves further investigation because that seems to be the major source of misunderstanding with the public and our clients. No agent is expected to perform tasks or to know information that is outside the scope of responsibility conferred by his or her real estate license. As noted earlier, licensees are not expected to be engineers, contractors, accountants, or lawyers. They are expected to be able to help clients obtain competent advice in the areas where they do not have the necessary expertise. However, agents are obligated to have knowledge and expertise regarding the properties being considered and also information about the neighborhood and the community that would help the buyer make an informed purchase decision. Facts such as zoning regulations, development in the vicinity, taxes, schools, and public transportation are all necessary elements of the agent's knowledge base.

It is critical that you competently answer every inquiry of your principal. If you do not know the answer, just say so; but then you must find the answer from a reliable source. Do not guess or speculate, because your client's question is frequently the very issue that later becomes a dispute. It is very common to hear a client say, "I relied completely on what my agent told me." Don't get caught in that trap!

Accounting

The duty of accounting for all funds and property under the agent's control primarily deals with the trust account aspect of fiduciary responsibility. Agents are considered to have a responsibility to several different people in the handling and disposition of earnest money deposits. For instance, when an earnest money deposit is received with an offer, to whom does it really belong—the buyer or the seller? Actually, it could belong to either one, and usually for some period of time, if there are contingencies, it will belong to both parties.

As a buyer's agent, you must be particularly careful to see that your client's interests are protected with regard to the earnest money. If you do not deposit the funds in your own escrow account, which may be precluded by local custom, policy, or regulation, then you must be assured that the broker or escrow agent holding the deposit is reliable and trustworthy.

Other items to be escrowed also could be placed under the agent's control. All of these monies or property must be carefully accounted for and reported to the principal. In regard to a formal escrow, there must be a written and signed escrow agreement to protect all parties—in particular, the agent.

SUMMARY

Buyers who are represented by buyers' agents automatically become clients rather than customers. Such buyers are also called *principals*. Because of this client relationship, the buyer's agent owes fiduciary/statutory duties to the principal.

These fiduciary duties include (1) loyalty, (2) disclosure, (3) confidentiality, (4) obedience, (5) reasonable care and diligence, and (6) accounting for all items of value. These are similar to the fiduciary duties owed to a seller principal; they are absolute, and their performance will be enforced by any court of law.

REVIEW QUESTIONS

1. John, a salesperson for Mountain Realty, is searching through the computer for some available properties to show Mary. He finds a property he listed, one another sales agent in his office listed, one in the MLS listed by another company, and a FSBO.

   a. How does he explain to Mary who he represents for each of these properties?

   b. Does it matter how the properties are listed?

ANSWERS:

   a. The answers can vary depending on whether or not state statute allows the practice of designated brokerage and/nonagency.

   For John's listing, he would be a seller's agent and treat Mary as a customer or, if allowed, he could do nonagency that would require switching the seller from agency to nonagency. As another alternative, he could, if allowed, represent the seller and designate another agent in his office to represent Mary.

   For the company listing, he would represent Mary unless the seller had been listed as nonagency in which case he would have to work with Mary as a nonagent.

   For the MLS listing, he would represent Mary, or if allowed, he could work with her as a nonagent regardless of how the seller was listed.

   For the FSBO, the answer would be the same as for the MLS listing provided he made full disclosure to the seller of his agency/nonagency status. A buyer's agent should not attempt to list the FSBO as that would create an unnecessary conflict of interest.

b. How the properties are listed only makes a difference if the listing is John's or his company's. See above for details.

2. A buyer's agent is potentially liable to the buyer for all of the following *EXCEPT*
   a. failing to show a buyer a nearby comparable FSBO property that is a better deal than the one the buyer bought.
   b. buying for the broker's own account a comparable property not disclosed to the buyer.
   c. failing to disclose to a buyer that the seller is rumored to have AIDS.
   d. disclosing to a seller that a buyer has two secret options on adjoining parcels.

ANSWER:

c. Buyers' agents must disclose all material facts, such as items (a) and (b), to the buyer with the exception of facts that cannot be disclosed by law such as item (c). The buyer agent must not disclose any confidential information about the buyer to the seller such as item (d).

3. Duties of a seller's agent/nonagent to a buyer include
   a. "caveat emptor."
   b. nondisclosure of structural problems.
   c. providing fair and honest information.
   d. full fiduciary duties.

ANSWER:

c.   Fair and honest treatment is the duty owed to all consumers whether client or customer. Choice (a) means "buyer beware" and disappeared when disclosure laws required disclosure of all material facts; (b) is illegal; (d) is owed only to clients, and a buyer working with either the seller's agent or a nonagent would be a customer.

4. A principal, in order to create a fiduciary relationship, *MUST*
   a.   consent.
   b.   sign a written contract.
   c.   pay a fee.
   d.   buy real estate.

ANSWER:

a.   It is not necessary for a principal to pay a fee (c) or buy real estate (d) in order to enter a fiduciary relationship. The principal must, however, give consent. In some states, it is also necessary to sign a written agreement. In those states, such as Colorado, both (a) and (b) would be correct; in all other states, only (a) is correct.

5. An agent, in order to create a fiduciary relationship, *MUST*
   a.   consent.
   b.   act on behalf of the principal.
   c.   be subject to the principal's control.
   d.   All of the above

ANSWER:

d. Agents who enter a fiduciary relationship must do (a), (b), and (c); therefore, (d) is the correct answer.

6. Customers are buyers
    a. an agent works for.
    b. to whom an agent owes fair and honest treatment.
    c. to whom an agent owes fiduciary duties.
    d. for whom an agent acts as an advocate.

ANSWER:

b. Agents owe fair and honest treatment to all consumers, including customers; (a), (c), and (d) apply only to clients.

7. Clients are buyers who are
    a. principals.
    b. represented by an agent.
    c. owed fiduciary duties.
    d. All of the above

ANSWER:

d. Clients are principals, represented by an agent who owes them fiduciary duties. Therefore (d) is the correct answer.

8. Which is *NOT* a fiduciary duty?
    a. Equality of treatment
    b. Loyalty
    c. Confidentiality
    d. Obedience

ANSWER:

a. Equality of treatment is a requirement of fair housing laws; it is not a fiduciary duty. Answers (b) and (d) are fiduciary duties along with reasonable skill and care, disclosure, and accounting.

9. Having a conflict of interest with a client would violate which fiduciary duty?
   a. Disclosure
   b. Obedience
   c. Loyalty
   d. Reasonable care and diligence

ANSWER:

a. Loyalty means putting the client's interests above those of all others, including the agent's. A conflict of interest means that the agent has someone else's interests in mind as well. Should this situation occur, the conflict must be disclosed to the client, and a solution found.

10. The duty of disclosure requires that an agent disclose all of the following *EXCEPT*
    a. facts that might affect the principal's decision.
    b. information outside the scope of the agent's licensed authority.
    c. information the agent would be expected to know.
    d. personal information known by the agent and material to the client.

ANSWER:

b.   An agent is not expected or required to disclose information outside the scope of his or her licensed authority because such information would probably not be reliable. However, (a), (c), and (d) must all be disclosed.

11. Which buyers should be treated as customers rather than clients?
    a.   Those who ask the agent to act unethically
    b.   Those with whom the agent has a personality clash
    c.   Some very experienced buyers who prefer to be treated as customers
    d.   All of the above

ANSWER:

d.   (a), (b), and (c) are all buyers who should not be taken on as clients; therefore, the correct answer is (d); (a) and (b) should probably be referred to another agent.

12. The buyer's agent can act in which of the following manners without violating fiduciary duties?
    a.   As an advocate for the seller
    b.   As an advocate for the buyer
    c.   As an advocate for both the buyer and the seller
    d.   None of the above

ANSWER:

b.   Either (a) or (c) would be a conflict of interest for a buyer's agent. A buyer's agent must be the advocate for his or her client.

13. A conflict of interest can occur when
    a. the agent's personal interest takes precedence over that of his or her principal's best interest.
    b. the agent practices consensual dual agency.
    c. Both
    d. Neither

ANSWER:

   c. Both (a) and (b) are conflicts of interest.

CASE STUDY:
Disclosure and Confidentiality

Sam Attaboy had listed Sally Adamant's vintage home. Bob Careful made a purchase offer that was contingent on a home inspection. The home inspection disclosed that the gas furnace was in need of replacement because unacceptable levels of carbon monoxide were being emitted.

Based on the home inspector's report, Bob chose not to proceed with the purchase.

Sam told Sally that the condition of the furnace and the risk that it posed to the home's inhabitants would need to be disclosed to other potential purchasers. Sally disagreed and instructed Sam not to say anything about the furnace to other potential purchasers. Sam replied that was an instruction he could not follow so Sam and Sally terminated the listing agreement.

Three months later, Sam noticed that Sally's home was back on the market, this time listed with Harry Goodboy. His curiosity piqued, Sam phoned Harry and asked whether there was a new furnace in the home. "Why no," said Harry. "Why do you ask?" Sam told Harry about the home inspector's earlier findings and suggested that Harry check with the seller to see if repairs had been made.

When Harry raised the question with Sally, Sally was irate. "That's none of his business," said Sally who became even angrier when Harry advised her that potential purchasers would have to be told about the condition of the furnace since it posed a serious potential health risk.

Sally filed an ethics complaint against Sam alleging that the physical condition of her property was confidential; that Sam had an ongoing duty to respect confidential information gained in the course of their relationship; and that Sam had breached Sally's confidence by sharing information about the furnace with Harry.

   a. Do Sam and Harry have a duty to disclose the carbon monoxide levels to prospective buyers?

   b. What kinds of information must be disclosed?

   c. What kinds of information must be kept confidential?

ANSWERS:

   a. Sam and Harry each have a duty to disclose to any buyer the material facts each knows about Sally's home, including the levels of carbon monoxide discovered by the inspector.

   b. All material facts about a property must be disclosed.

   c. Confidential type information obtained during an agency relationship must be kept confidential unless permission to disclose is obtained from the party whose information it is. Confidential information would include highest price a buyer would pay, motivation, and so on.

CHAPTER 3

Buyer Clients and Their Needs

WHO ARE BUYER CLIENTS?

Many buyers should be clients because of some existing or prior relationship. Not treating such buyers as clients can potentially result in undisclosed dual agency. Let's look at some of these situations.

- **The licensee buying for his or her own account**
  If the agent is also the purchaser (and particularly if he or she is receiving a commission from the transaction), it is virtually impossible for the licensee not to be his or her own agent. To help avoid agency problems when buying for your own account, do not accept a commission. To be extra safe, hire another agent or an attorney to represent you. Of course, you must disclose that you are a licensed agent and, furthermore, that you are representing yourself and not the seller.

- **A buyer who requires anonymity**

  Any buyer who desires to remain anonymous must be a buyer client, because a seller's agent/subagent is required to disclose to the seller the buyer's identity.

- **A relative of the licensee**

  This category includes any relative, such as a spouse, brother, sister, brother-in-law, sister-in-law, mother, father, mother-in-law, father-in-law, cousin, aunt, uncle, nephew, niece, and, in general, anyone considered to be a relative by either blood or marriage.

- **A close friend**

  This designation applies to any person whom you have known well for some time and whose relationship with you is recognized as a close friendship by others. Some examples include school roommates, fraternity brothers or sorority sisters or members of a club, group, or church that you meet with on a regular basis. In essence, it could be anyone whom you consider and who considers you to be a good friend.

- **A business associate or partner**

  This is any person with whom you have a business relationship who would normally expect you to serve as his or her agent. This category would probably not include limited partners whom you do not know well or other employees of a large company.

- **Former clients**

  Former clients, whether buyers or sellers, would be likely to consider you as their agent. Because licensees are special agents and not general agents, it is usually acceptable to treat former seller clients as buyer customers, provided that you make a full and proper disclosure.

However, because you probably know a great deal about a former client, it is difficult, if not impossible, not to continue to treat him or her as a client because, once he or she becomes a customer, you would need to disclose what you know about the former client to your new client. Customers are not entitled to confidentiality as is a client.

■ **Any buyer who definitely wants his or her own agent** These buyers are usually people who have had some exposure to real estate practice and understand the typical seller agency situation. These people understand what the word *agency* means and want to have an advocate on their team.

It should be clear by now that any buyer in one of the categories described above ought to be treated as a client. Common sense suggests that buyers in all of these categories, most of whom do not understand real estate agency, will just assume that you are acting on their behalf and in their best interests. If the decision is made that they will be customers and a full disclosure is done, there will inevitably still be some exposure to misunderstanding and misrepresentation. Even when a full and understandable disclosure is made, it will be awkward for most buyers in any of the relationships described not to request and expect client status.

WHY BUYERS NEED TO BE REPRESENTED

Let's consider for a moment two additional major categories of homebuyers: *first-time buyers* and *out-of-town buyers* (e.g., corporate transferees). The first-time buyer knows nothing about buying a home, financing, what he or she can afford, the market, or many other issues. The newcomer does not know the market, pricing, or other information about the community. People in both of these categories need help from someone they can trust who will look out for their best interests. They need advice and advocacy, two primary characteristics of an agency relationship. In the commercial arena, there are corporate relocations, tenants moving into town, and out-of-state investors, all of whom need special help and representation.

None of this is meant to minimize the importance of the seller. However, the seller is almost always represented by his or her own agent and has the following special needs:

- **Marketing the property**
  While this is no simple task, the process is relatively routine, with generally standard procedures for advertising, providing MLS exposure, preparing brochures and signs, pricing the property, and executing other activities. The primary objective of the listing is to expose the property to the largest number of qualified potential buyers. Certainly, listing agents vary in ability, but the basic services they offer do not change that much.

- **Negotiating for the highest price and the best terms**
  This task is an important component of the listing process and definitely commands the highest level of skill and experience that the agent has to offer. It may well be the most important service the listing agent has to provide for the seller.

- **Managing the closing process**
  Once again, this is a relatively routine procedure that relies to a large extent on the services of other professionals,

such as closing or escrow agents, loan processors, and inspectors.

Buyers' Specific Needs

Now, let's take a look at the buyer's needs.

Information about the Community and the Real Estate Market. Buyers, particularly those new to the community, need information in order to make a decision about where in the community they want to live and/or work.

Access to the Entire Marketplace. Buyers generally want to see every property that might meet their criteria. Even if they do not see everything, they rely on the agent to help them determine what is best for them. This is a big responsibility, and the agent working for the buyer should not be restricted by any company policy, listing limitation, or special incentive that may affect a seller's agent/subagent or nonagent.

Selection of a Property and Preparation of an Offer. At this point, the buyer really needs an advocate and a counselor. The seller's agent/subagent, who must be extremely careful about giving advice, must not recommend a price and terms for the offer other than those already offered by the seller. The agent's ability to write a good contract with all of the necessary provisions is very important to the buyer (see Chapter 9).

Negotiation for the Lowest Price and Best Terms. Most buyers, whether clients or customers, believe that their salesperson is trying to get them the best price and terms when, in reality, licensees other than buyers' agents cannot be their advocate in negotiations with the seller. However, a buyer's agent must act as the buyer's advocate, negotiator, and advisor.

Verification of Value. A buyer should know that he or she is paying a reasonable and fair price for the property. A buyer's agent can perform a comparative market analysis (CMA) to determine the market value of the property and then suggest an appropriate price to pay. Seller agents/subagents must be very cautious about this procedure and must not recommend any price other than the listing price without the seller's permission. Yet it is impractical to suggest that such agents should not provide the buyer customers with information about value. When asked, they can respond appropriately in three ways:

1. Prepare a CMA that legitimately indicates a value equal to or greater than the list price
2. Request a copy of the listing agent's CMA
3. Give the buyer a printout of all the properties that have sold in the general area, without providing any analysis whatsoever

Knowledge of Available Financing. This is an important service that most buyers need. They must know the loan amount for which they can qualify, where to go to get the best terms, and what the loan is going to cost them. Buyers' agents must know the financial marketplace so that they can advise buyers where to get the best loan at the lowest rates and the lowest cost. Other agents can also provide this service, usually without jeopardizing their agency status, but they need to be careful about eliciting confidential information. When owner financing is available, seller agents/subagents must be especially careful not to compromise their agency duties.

Verification of Property Condition. The buyer must be assured that the property is in sound condition and that the systems are all operating properly. It is important to know what will be done if something is wrong with the property or if something happens to it before closing. Most contracts will cover this contingency, but the buyer must be well informed about the remedies and options available.

Buyers need to be advised about the ramifications of a property inspection, how to have it done, how much it will cost, and what to do about any defects that are discovered. Once again, seller's agents/subagents must be careful about how they handle these situations to avoid violating their duty to the seller. In contrast, buyers' agents can be very assertive in representing the buyer and in requesting that deficiencies be corrected by the seller.

Verification of Clear Title. The buyer needs assurance of a clear title to the property he or she is buying. This will usually involve lawyers and abstracts or title companies. All agents must be very careful about giving legal advice in this area. *Defects* or *clouds* on the title account for a large number of the problems that arise in real estate transactions, and all agents must be aware of and alert to this potential pitfall.

Determination of Adequate Zoning. Every buyer must know that the property he or she is buying is properly zoned for the intended use. Is the property a nonconforming use or is it under a special use permit that may apply only to the existing owner and cannot be transferred or assigned? Is the property subject to some existing restrictive covenants? All agents must be prepared to answer these questions or, at the very least, know where to find the answers. Zoning questions are especially important in commercial transactions, where the use, or intended use, of the property is of critical importance to the buyer. All agents must be familiar with current zoning ordinances in their communities.

Access to the Property. Access is not usually a problem in improved, subdivided urban areas and incorporated cities. However, it can be a major consideration for buyers of raw ground or of isolated parcels that are some distance from any major street or highway. Frequently, the only access to a property is via an easement, and it is critical that the easement document be properly written and recorded.

Verification of Property Boundaries. Buyers must know exactly what property they are buying. In most urban properties with residential improvements, the boundaries are usually obvious because lot lines are delineated by fences, roads, or other physical means. However, in any unimproved or large vacant land parcel or commercial property, the boundaries may not be obvious and problems can arise. Often, even the current owners of properties do not know exactly where the lot lines are and feel quite surprised to discover that what they actually own is quite different from what they thought they owned.

A survey is almost always required by lenders and probably should be included in all transactions. This document should be reviewed by the attorney, and it should delineate all easements and any encroachments on the property. For an analysis of future salability, a buyer needs to know whether his or her investment is reasonably secure. Will the property under consideration retain its value, or is there a possibility of something happening that could cause a loss of value? The buyer's agent is able to point out any problems that would affect the future marketing of the property and comment on whether or not the property will appreciate in value. These considerations are fairly subjective, and they will test the agent's knowledge of the market and general experience in the business. However, most buyers will ask questions, and agents must be able to answer them intelligently. In these situations, the buyer's agent has complete freedom to provide honest opinions without the fear of violating any duty to the seller.

Management of the Closing Process. This step is just as important to the buyer as it is to the seller. However, a big difference is that the seller is not concerned with the new loan being sought by the buyer. Obtaining this loan and closing it make up an important part of the buyer's activities and concerns in the closing process. The buyer's agent will usually take a much more active role than would other agents in assisting the buyer in the entire closing process.

Preservation of the Buyer's Anonymity. For various reasons, some buyers wish to remain anonymous. Frequently, well-known or famous people or large corporations or institutions do not want their identity known during the real estate negotiation process. Sometimes knowledge of the potential purchaser's identity and financial capability can prevent the buyer from getting the best possible deal. The practice of working with a broker as a nominee for the buyer is common when an individual or group is trying to create an assemblage of property. The agent or subagent of the seller must disclose the identity of the buyer, whereas the agent of the buyer is legitimately able to maintain the client's anonymity.

SUMMARY

It should be apparent by now that the buyer in a real estate transaction requires help with a greater variety of tasks than does the seller. Many of these needs will be satisfied by others such as lenders, inspectors, surveyors, and lawyers, but buyers need competent advice and counsel on where to get help in all of these areas. A buyer's agent has much more freedom to advise and recommend solutions to the buyer than do other agents, who must be careful about giving advice, particularly if it could jeopardize the seller's position in the transaction. First-time buyers or buyers inexperienced in a specific area or with a particular type of property usually look to their agent for competent and reliable help. It is very difficult for a licensee to perform all of the necessary tasks well and not be considered the agent of the buyer, at least in the buyer's own mind.

As has been mentioned before, when the behavior of a seller's agent/subagent or a nonagent parallels that of an advocate for the buyer, an undisclosed dual agency situation can arise, and that is very risky indeed.

REVIEW QUESTIONS

1. Which buyer must be a client rather than a customer?
   a. Business colleague
   b. Corporate transferee
   c. First-time buyer
   d. One who requires anonymity

ANSWER:

d. Choices (a), (b), and (c) can be treated as customers with great care; (a) because you probably know confidential information that would have to be disclosed to the seller; (b) because they need assistance with value; and (c) because they usually need help with everything and tend to rely on their agent. However, an agent can only provide anonymity to a client through the fiduciary duty of confidentiality.

2. Assume Broker Fred is purchasing a two-bedroom condominium unit for his own investment account. The purchase of which one of the following properties would involve the least risk of dual agency conflict for Fred?
   a. In-house listing of another sales agent in another branch office
   b. One of Fred's listings
   c. Listing on the MLS
   d. An FSBO property

ANSWER:

c. MLS listings are usually arm's-length transactions so that any agency conflict would be minimized. However, Fred's own listing, unless listed as a nonagency relationship, is an agency relationship and Fred has to represent himself. The same rationale would apply to a company listing. An FSBO should be treated as a customer but, unless the FSBO is represented by an attorney, all the assistance he or she usually needs runs the risk of creating an agency conflict.

3. Which buyer should not be accepted as a buyer client?
    a. One who prefers to be treated as a customer
    b. One who wants anonymity
    c. A close friend
    d. A relative

ANSWER:

   a.   Buyers who prefer to be treated as customers should be allowed to do so and not accepted as clients. However, because subagency is not done in most states, this would require entering a nonagency relationship if allowed by your state. In some states like Nebraska, however, the law presumes that an agency relationship exists.

4

Buyer Agency Is Business as Usual

As occurs with any other relationship, buyer agency results in both benefits and liabilities for the buyer, the buyer's agent, the seller, the seller's agent, and the real estate industry in general. However, when correctly practiced, buyer agency in combination with seller agency results in more benefits and fewer liabilities for everyone. A more even balance between buyer and seller, in turn, tends to yield true win-win transactions and an environment with fewer causes for lawsuits.

BENEFITS FOR THE BUYER

As a client who has a contract with the agent, the buyer should receive the agent's total commitment, effort, and confidentiality. Because this is a relationship of choice, both parties should find common trust and respect. Together, the buyer and the agent can find the best solutions to the buyer's needs and wants as they work in an atmosphere of mutual honesty. The buyer client can relax, knowing that his or her interests are being represented by that agent to all other agents and sellers.

Because the buyer's agent is not restrained by reason of commission to properties listed on the MLS, the buyer client has a larger market from which to choose and is thus more likely to find just the "right" property. In addition to MLS listings, the buyer has access to unlisted properties, including both those for-sale-by-owner and those with no hint that the owner desires a sale. This latter category is especially important in markets where demand exceeds supply.

Regardless of the property source, once the purchase offer is written, the buyer client is assured the strongest possible negotiating position, because of the advice, advocacy, and representation that the agent provides. This strong position is critical twice: initially, in negotiating contract terms beneficial to the buyer, and later, in managing the closing process. Bringing a transaction to closing involves moving through a maze of interrelated events—loan qualification, appraisal, survey, title work, inspections, occupancy—each with its own due date and significance. A missed date or unacceptable results reopen negotiations, requiring a timely response made in the buyer's best interest.

Only buyer clients can remain anonymous, since selling agents who represent the seller must disclose the buyer's identity to the seller. Although anonymity is not important to most buyers, it is a critical factor to those whose negotiating position would be damaged by knowledge of their identity. To such buyers, the client status available only through buyer agency is of utmost importance.

Because the buyer usually is the ultimate source of all transaction funds, buyers, customers, and clients alike pay the agent commissions. However, as is readily apparent by the above discussion, only buyer clients receive full value for the commission paid.

LIABILITIES FOR THE BUYER

The biggest liability is choosing the wrong agent. As is true of any other profession, the ability of practitioners (agents) varies from excellent to moderate to poor and, because market forces tend to determine fees, there is rarely any economic benefit in choosing less than the best. Buyers should, therefore, select their agent based on general reputation, specific referrals, and personal interviews.

Personal interviews are the most important of these three. During the interview, the buyer should ask for a description of the planned services, experience statistics for the agent and the company, and the individual's relevant education and training. While listening to the answers, the buyer should be sensitive to the respondent's enthusiasm and general attitude. Is the agent someone to be trusted and respected? If possible, the buyer should interview two or three agents before making a commitment to one.

A second potential liability is based on the company's agency policy. Determine what will happen if the buyer decides to purchase a company listing. Does the company have a single agency policy requiring that either the buyer or the seller be referred to another company to complete the transaction? Does the company have a dual agency policy in which it would represent both parties? This would not be possible for states that have eliminated dual agency. Or does the company use nonagency for in-house transactions, requiring that both (buyer and seller) agency relationships be terminated? Regardless of the policy, can the agent answer all your questions satisfactorily? How do you feel about the policy?

Finally, one less important but related liability remains. Some institutional sellers, including the FHA in the sale of its repossessed properties, and some builders require that the seller alone be represented. In this regard, the buyer must determine the likelihood of purchasing a property from such a seller. As there is little probability of changing the stance of such sellers, the buyer generally must accept that he or she cannot obtain client-level representation when purchasing from such sellers.

BENEFITS FOR THE AGENT

For agents, the primary benefit is buyer loyalty, which results in a satisfying, open, working relationship based on trust and mutual respect. Buyer agency thus removes the fear that other agents may "steal" your buyer. Because the buyer is listed, you will be motivated to work harder for the buyer: you have an incentive to show the buyer every relevant property. This, in turn, generally yields more income because you waste less time, get more referrals, and retain more repeat clients.

Closely related to these advantages is the ethical peace of mind you will feel as you avoid the conflict of interest between buyer and seller that you might otherwise feel in a buyer customer relationship.

Last, but certainly not least, is that buyer agency is one more service you can offer to prospective clients. Each time you and your company can add another service to your "tool kit," your income potential increases.

LIABILITIES FOR THE AGENT

The agent's liabilities in buyer agency are primarily psychological. As is true of any change, there will be discomfort: for most people, it is simply easier and more comfortable to continue doing what they have always done.

In addition, however, some time and money will be spent on education. Similarly, additional time will be required to generate a sufficient client base and reputation as an expert buyer's agent.

There is, of course, legal liability to the buyer client, just as the listing agent has legal liability to the seller. Buyers' agents owe duties either statutory or fiduciary to their clients, and if any breach should occur, there is liability. The potential for serious consequences includes rescission of the contract, lost commission, punitive damages, loss of license, and so on.

Liability can be very large in some markets and some offices and insignificant in others. Because buyer agency is "business as usual" in most markets, defensiveness, conflict, and mistrust are less likely to develop between listing agents and buyers' agents. This situation is best dealt with via education by neutral trainers, who are not zealots for either position, and who encourage open communication between listing and buyers' agents.

BENEFITS FOR THE LISTING AGENT AND THE SELLER

Benefits for the listing agent and seller can be quite simply stated: a buyer client tends to be more controlled and better prepared than a buyer customer. It is easier, more efficient, and more businesslike to deal with a buyer who is realistic and well advised.

As a result of buyer agency, the loyalties and responsibilities of all involved brokers are clear. Although the listing agent and the seller may not like the fact that the buyer is represented, there is a real benefit to knowing who represents whom, as there is substantially less liability exposure for both sellers and listing agents when a buyer agent is involved.

LIABILITIES FOR THE LISTING AGENT AND THE SELLER

The greatest liability for the listing agent and the seller is, of course, having to deal with a tough negotiator who is working on behalf of the buyer. This does, however, create the potential for a fairer outcome for all parties to the transaction that is less likely to result in future lawsuits.

Perhaps the worst liability, especially for the listing agent, is the potential misuse of buyer agency by a few unethical and greedy buyers' agents. Such agents may try to take advantage of a seller who "has" to sell. Likewise, these agents may take advantage of the listing agent by abusing the rules of procuring cause. However, in such cases, often the perceived misuse or abuse is simply legal representation combined with some degree of listing agent fear.

BENEFITS AND LIABILITIES FOR THE REAL ESTATE INDUSTRY

The benefits offered by seller agency/buyer agency cannot be underestimated, for it clearly introduces greater fairness into real estate transactions. In turn, fairer transactions are perceived as win-win situations and are less likely to result in lawsuits.

Simultaneously, when both parties to a transaction are treated as clients, the level of professionalism is likely to increase, because awareness of client-level fiduciary duties will also increase.

SUMMARY

The widespread introduction of buyer agency into any market has had both benefits and liabilities for each of the players involved. However, overall, it is apparent that the benefits far outweigh the liabilities.

REVIEW QUESTIONS

1. Buyers' agents should
   a. demand excessive fees.
   b. go around the listing agent.
   c. ignore association and MLS rules as they only apply to listing agents.
   d. None of the above

ANSWER:

d. None of the answers should be done by any buyer's agent; the answer is (d).

2. A benefit of buyer agency for the buyer is
    a. having an advocate during negotiations.
    b. selecting the wrong agent.
    c. difficulty in changing agents.
    d. uncooperative listing agents.

ANSWER:

a. Choices (b), (c), and (d) are not benefits to buyer clients; they are liabilities. Having an advocate is the strongest benefit of buyer agency and is therefore the correct answer. Advocacy is not available from nonagents.

3. A buyer client is much more likely to
    a. make sure that arrangements are made to ensure that the agent is paid.
    b. not pay attention to the details of the transaction.
    c. not communicate with the agent.
    d. fail to return phone calls.

ANSWER:

a. Buyer clients usually have close relationships with their buyer's agent. As a result they usually do not do (b), (c), and/ or (d). Because of the buyer counseling session, buyer clients are knowledgeable about how their agents are paid and are much more likely to ensure that the agents are paid.

5

How to Decide if You Want to Be a Buyer's Agent

Whether or not to represent buyers depends on several factors, some of which make buyer agency mandatory or at least strongly suggested while others make it optional, a choice on the part of both agent and buyer. These factors include the company's policy on agency, the relationship between agent and buyer, and time requirements.

COMPANY AGENCY POLICY

For reasons of both liability and efficiency, every real estate company should have a clear policy on agency that is well understood and followed by its agents. Such a policy, which is essential for adequate risk management, is established when the broker, his or her advisors, and the company's agents answer the following questions:

- What is our current practice?
- Based on our risk tolerance and estimate of potential business loss, which of the possible agency policies would we prefer to have?
- What conflict, if any, is there between our current practice and the agency policy we would prefer?
- How can we eliminate these areas of conflict?
- What brokerage relationships are allowed under the law (policy can't do anything contrary to the law); which relationships do we want to practice?

Assuming that the areas of conflict are eliminated, the elected policy can be implemented by means of forms, brochures, training and supervision of agents, and a standard agency disclosure to both clients and customers.

Whether or not you can practice buyer agency thus first depends on whether your company allows it. Of the four possible policies listed below, only the first does not permit buyer agency. Thus, to practice buyer agency, you must work in a firm that has elected policy number 2, 3, or 4.

1. **Seller agency exclusively, whether listing or selling.** Buyers are always treated as customers and sellers are always represented by the listing agent and his or her sales agents.
2. **Buyer agency exclusively.** Only buyers are represented; potential sellers are referred to another company.
3. **Single agency, whether listing or selling.** The broker and his or her agents can represent either the seller or the buyer, but not both in the same transaction. Should a buyer client want to purchase an in-house listing, one

of the clients (seller or buyer) may be referred to another company or the buyer agency may be terminated. Because the steps needed to preclude such a situation are possible only in very small, well-disciplined companies, this policy is normally used only in companies with fewer than three to five agents.

4. **Consensual dual agency/designated agency/ nonagency[1] for in-house sales and single agency (either buyer or seller) otherwise.** (Which of these three possibilities is elected depends on what is allowed by your state regulations and/or statute; a broker's firm can only practice that which is legally allowed by regulation and/or statute.) Buyers are always treated as clients, as are sellers. During the initial counseling session, the agent discloses the potential for an in-house sale should a buyer client want to purchase a seller client's property and obtains the client's informed consent for such dual agency. Because a well-implemented policy of disclosed dual agency/designated agency/nonagency may present less risk than the potential of an undisclosed dual agency that could occur under policy number 1 or 3, many offices, especially larger ones, elect this policy.

Although having a stated policy on agency is desirable and, in some states, mandatory, many companies still do not have one. In such a circumstance, should any agent practice buyer agency and sell an in-house listing, the broker and the

---

1. Although definitions vary from state to state, all include the inability of nonagents to be advocates for any party to the transaction. This inability removes the most important opportunities for adding value to the transaction; for this reason nonagency practice is not expected to be a major factor in the future.

firm effectively have a policy of undisclosed dual agency—a very risky policy! Unfortunately, this practice is still characteristic of some of today's firms, which claim to practice seller agency only, yet allow agents who either want or need to represent a buyer to do so. Such firms thus have, by default, a policy of undisclosed dual agency whenever one of their buyer clients purchases or even shows interest in a company listing.

Clearly, a far less risky management decision is to elect one of the policies that allows the practice of buyer agency. However, the only truly effective policy is number 4: dual agency/designated brokerage/nonagency for in-house sales and single agency (either buyer or seller) otherwise. This statement is substantiated in practice by data collected in a 1990 California Association of REALTORS® survey of California real estate firms. When asked what agency relationship was chosen when the agent's firm was both listing and cooperating selling broker/agent, 92 percent responded that they represented both the buyer and seller and only 4 percent that they represented the seller exclusively.

For practitioners and their legal advisors, managing in-house sales can at first appear quite frightening and very risky. However, after careful consideration of the alternatives, many brokers have decided that given adequate forms and contracts as well as a trained staff, a policy of disclosed dual agency/designated brokerage/nonagency for in-house sales is the only practical way of allowing their agents to both list property and represent buyers. The key to such a policy is a thorough discussion between agents and their clients about in-house sales, the possible alternatives, and the ramifications in terms of both agent and client behavior and responsibilities should dual agency/designated brokerage/nonagency occur. To be effective, such discussions must take place and informed consent must be obtained when a seller client signs the listing contract and a buyer client signs the buyer agency agreement. Examples of dual agency disclosure amendments for both buyer and seller are in the forms appendix at the end of this book.

For an in-depth discussion of the agency policies, their implications, and their implementation, an old but excellent 1988 book by John Reilly and Michael Somers, titled *Agency Disclosure: The Complete Office Policy Guide* (Real Estate Video Educational Institute, Calabasas, Calif.) is recommended. Another text, *Consensual Dual Agency: A Practical Approach to the In-House Sale,* by Harlan, Lyons, and Reilly, extensively deals with the practice of disclosed, consensual dual agency and the policies and procedures necessary to its effective, legal practice.

RELATIONSHIP BETWEEN AGENT AND BUYER

As previously outlined (see Chapter 3), there are several types of people who either must or should be treated as buyer clients.

- **Must**
  Agent buying for his or her own account
  Buyer who requires anonymity
- **Should**
  Relative
  Close friend
  Business associate or partner
  Former clients and/or customers

First-time buyer

Out-of-town buyer

Buyer who wants to be represented

An agent who wishes to treat buyers on the "should" list as customers must exercise great skill. In the absence of a very specific disclosure to the contrary, these buyers would reasonably assume that they are being represented. The only way for the agent to prevent such an assumption would be to make a clear statement about his or her role as a representative of the seller or of neither party and to reinforce that disclosure with words and actions while working with the buyer. In other words, buyers on the "should" list expect to be represented. It is easier for the agent to treat those buyers as clients.

Many experienced agents always elect to treat another group of buyers as customers or refer them to another company. These are the buyers with whom there is a personality clash. For you, this category may consist of people who are so difficult to work with that they cause you to suffer great frustration and even anger. They may be people who insist that you act unethically or illegally, or they may simply be those with whom you are uncomfortable. In any case, because they are not people to whom you could easily be loyal and obedient, it would be difficult if not impossible to have them as clients. It can be a sign of great maturity when you elect not to work with such a buyer.

Finally, some buyers simply prefer to be treated as customers and will not elect client status. They generally fall into three categories: (1) those who want to retain the right to work with more than one agent, (2) those very experienced buyers who truly do not need representation, and (3) those who are comfortable with what they perceive to be the status quo and are uncomfortable with change.

During the initial counseling session (see Chapter 8), if you are an agent who prefers to act as a buyer's representative, you should be especially sensitive to the buyers described above who either would be difficult to treat as clients or do not want client status. You must decide as soon as possible whether to work with such buyers as customers (which should depend at least in part on company policy) or to refer them to another agent.

AGENT EXPERTISE

Your expertise in both the type of property and general geographic location of the property is also critical. Even though you are licensed to sell any kind of property located anywhere within the state whose regulatory agency licensed you, your expertise from a practical standpoint is far more limited.

Remember that, as a buyer's agent, you are the expert for your buyer client. Therefore, you must have sufficient knowledge about both the property type and location that interests the client so that you can advise as to value and any idiosyncrasies relative to that type of property. Should a client want property about which you are not expert, refer the client to someone who is expert. If you want to become expert, educate yourself and/or volunteer your time and effort to someone who can help you become so.

TIME REQUIREMENTS

As obvious as it may seem, whether you represent buyers or sellers, you should, before contracting to represent an additional client, review your current commitments to determine whether you have sufficient time to work with yet another client. Making decisions based on probable time available is yet another characteristic of competent, professional agents.

Buyer representation, in particular, requires a major time commitment. However, several means are available to reduce the agent's personal time while still providing the buyer with adequate representation. In particular, the support staff and professionals in related fields can provide some of the essential services. An administrative assistant can review the existing market in search of properties that meet the buyer's requirements, preview these properties, and then set up appointments for those that best suit the buyer's needs. In addition, the buyer can be referred to knowledgeable, ethical experts in the areas of mortgage finance, home inspection, title insurance, appraisal, real estate law, and other fields as necessary to complete the purchase transaction.

In many ways, if you are a buyer's agent, your role is like that of an orchestra conductor who organizes and manages the efforts of many other performers. Your responsibility is to make sure that each specialist completes his or her job in a timely and cost-effective manner, all to the benefit of the buyer. Along with the ability to make professional referrals comes the additional liability to refer the buyer to competent, effective experts. Lawsuits based on charges of incompetent or negligent referrals are certainly not unusual!

SUMMARY

Your decision to act as a buyer agent depends on several factors, among which are (1) whether the company's policy allows buyer representation and, if so, under what circumstances; (2) the existing relationship between you and the prospective buyer and whether both parties want to enter into a client relationship; and (3) your current time commitments.

REVIEW QUESTIONS

1. Whether or not you decide to be a buyer's agent depends on all but
   a. company agency policy.
   b. relationship with the buyer.
   c. agent's time commitments.
   d. MLS membership.

   ANSWER:

   d. The MLS cannot determine the agency relationships of members. However, what agency relationships can be offered is determined by company agency policy. An agent's relationship with the buyer strongly influences whether or not one will be a buyer's agent. As buyers usually require a lot of an agent's time, an agent should not take on a new buyer client if he or she is already too busy.

2. Sam Broeker is the broker/owner of Broeker Realty in the town of Kneedapolicyville. Sam recently attended an agency training seminar and now realizes that he needs to

develop a formal office policy on brokerage relationships. Broeker Realty has six full-time and four part-time sales agents. More information about Broeker Realty follows:

- Existing office policy on brokerage relationships: none
- Company goal for upcoming year: increasing revenues by 20 percent
- Existing revenue base: 65 percent from seller representation, 35 percent from buyer representation
- Agent training on brokerage relationships: required prelicensing education plus two agents have taken a seminar on buyer agency
- Type of representation practiced: all agents practice seller agency, four also practice buyer agency
- Kneedapolicyville has 50,000 residents. Consumers are generally aware of both buyer and seller agency but unfamiliar with nonagency. The market currently has one exclusive buyer agency company; two companies that practice buyer agency, seller agency, and disclosed dual agency; and several companies that practice exclusive seller agency.

a.   What type of office policy on brokerage relationships should Sam Broeker institute for Broeker Realty?

b.   Provide reasons why your response to (a) above is the most appropriate policy.

ANSWERS:

a. The appropriate policy would be to offer all the relationships necessary to satisfy the needs of Broeker's market customers—buyer agency, seller agency, and disclosed dual agency (and/or, if allowed by state regulation, nonagency and designated brokerage).

b. Eliminating any of the possible relationships could result in a loss of business. If the policy is properly conceived and adequate training and supervision are provided, there should be no increase in liability.

3. John is holding an open house on Mrs. Smith's property when he meets Bob, an interested buyer prospect.
   a. How can an unintended dual agency arise?
   b. Should John represent Bob? Can he?
   c. Will Bob be turned off when John discloses that he represents Mrs. Smith?

ANSWERS:

a. An unintended dual agency can occur if John fails to disclose to Bob that he is the agent of the seller and what he can and cannot do on Bob's behalf. He must also disclose all the possible brokerage relationships available to Bob.

b. If either consensual disclosed dual agency or designated brokerage are allowed in John's state and his company policy allows either or both, he could represent both Mrs. Smith and Bob. However, because he already has an agency relationship with Mrs. Smith it would be best to either treat Bob as a customer or refer him to another agent in John's office and do designated brokerage (if allowed). Dual agency is always risky.

c. Whether or not Bob is turned off depends largely on John's skills in making the disclosures and answering Bob's concerns.

4. Mrs. Smith wants John, her listing agent, to help her find a replacement home. She's interested in an in-house listing.

   a. Once a client always a client? Or, is Mrs. Smith now a buyer customer?

   b. Is dual agency an appropriate choice?

   c. Should in-house and outside MLS listings be treated differently?

ANSWERS:

   a. John could legally treat Mrs. Smith as a buyer customer. However, given his agency relationship with her as her listing agent, he probably knows confidential information about her that she would not want disclosed. It would be difficult and unrealistic for John not to continue his agency relationship.

   b. Given that Mrs. Smith is interested in an in-house listing, dual agency is an appropriate choice. Depending on state statute and company agency policy, nonagency or designated brokerage are also possible choices.

   c. Assuming that John and Mrs. Smith have elected buyer agency, John will have disclosed to Mrs. Smith the ramifications of dual agency (and designated brokerage and nonagency if allowed). This is a significant difference when compared with MLS listings in which John will act as an unfettered buyer's agent.

5. Mary calls John and requests assistance in helping her to find a new home in a better area.

   a. When should John determine what the working relationship with Mary will be?

   b. How does John determine his working relationship with Mary?

ANSWERS:

a. The brokerage relationship should be determined before any properties are shown.

b. Which brokerage relationship is dependent upon Mary's desires to have an advocate as well as company agency policy and state statute.

CASE STUDY

Jim Bond and Art Gordon are sales agents for Ace Realty. The company policy is buyer agency and seller agency with disclosed dual agency for in-house sales. Art has a seller client named Holly Thorn. Before Holly signed a listing contract, Art informed her that the company cooperated with both nonagents and buyers' agents and that any buyer's agent with whom she comes in contact will not be representing her. Art received Holly's permission to cooperate with nonagents and buyers' agents, and he provided her with a brochure on brokerage relationships.

Jim meets with Terese Erickson, a potential buyer client and makes a disclosure similar to Art's. Jim and Terese enter into a buyer representation agreement.

A few days later, Jim calls Terese to tell her about an MLS property that is listed with Best Realty. Jim tells her that he does not think that it exactly meets her needs, but she should look at it anyway because it might be available at a great price. Jim says, "The listing broker indicated that the seller might be willing to come way down on the price. I don't think the broker realized that I'm working for you as your buyer's agent."

Jim also shows Terese Holly's property, as it came close to her requirements. Jim tells Art that he has a buyer client interested in Holly's property. Art meets with Holly and explains the concept of dual agency. Holly agrees to dual agency for a potential transaction with Terese, so long as Art will still negotiate for her. Art agrees.

Jim meets with Terese to get her consent to dual agency. He tells her that he is familiar with the property and the seller, because he has shown the property several times as the seller's agent. Jim indicates that he has information about Holly's bargaining position that he was unable to share with previous buyer customers, but because Terese is a buyer client he owes fiduciary duties to her and is obligated to tell her anything that would improve her bargaining position. Jim proceeds to tell Terese all the relevant information he knows about Holly.

    a.   What mistakes has Art made?

    b.   What mistakes has Jim made?

ANSWERS:

a. Art agreed to negotiate for his seller client, Holly. As a dual agent, you cannot negotiate on behalf of either client. Any information known about the buyer's willingness to pay more, or the seller's willingness to take less, or information about motivation cannot be disclosed. However, any market analysis provided to one client must also be provided to the other client.

b. Any information Jim received from/about Holly while showing her property as a seller's agent is confidential. Confidentiality, in most states, lasts indefinitely. Such information, therefore, cannot be disclosed even to a buyer client like Terese.

CHAPTER 6

Residential Markets for Buyers' Agents

Take advantage of the opportunities offered by your local market by doing a market assessment based on current census data (*www.census.gov*). Select a market segment that fits your aptitude and/or experience, and then thoroughly research that segment, developing a database and laying out a business plan to make your special expertise in that niche known to consumers and colleagues alike.

To assist you in creating your plan, this chapter overviews today's major market segments. We'll look at the following categories of residential buyers: first-time, immigrants, relocation, second home/resort, FSBOs, credit-impaired, luxury, and the largest of today's demographic groups—seniors, baby boomers, and Gen Xers. Each of these has special needs that your plan should create strategies to target and fulfill. Like the "geographic farming" technique used by listing agents, your plan will be for "social farming" one or more of these segments.

FIRST-TIME BUYERS

In most markets, first-timers make up approximately 40 percent of all homebuyers. Most have scrimped and saved, have read lots of books and magazine articles about how to make a smart purchase, and have fantasies of what their first home will look like. In terms of demographics, most of these buyers are Gen Xers or immigrants (see greater detail on these segments later in this chapter).

Often their fantasies far exceed their financial abilities, which means one of your first jobs is to introduce these buyers to an experienced loan officer with a good "bedside manner," ideally one who is familiar with FHA, low or no down-payment plans, municipal grant programs, seller-assisted financing such as Nehemiah, and so on.

Your counseling is especially important with this group as you'll often have to educate them about the market, showing them what they can afford in the geographic area they want and, if that doesn't sufficiently match their dreams, taking them to lower-priced areas that do. Help them prioritize their wants and needs. Provide them with recent sold information and articles. Gain their trust by being patient, not pushing. Often it will take approximately six months to both educate and close; first-time buyers usually require a lot of hand-holding. Your biggest challenge is helping them understand what they can afford, including tax ramifications.

Everything is new to a first-timer. Be prepared with referrals to not only lenders but inspectors, painters, repair people, insurance agents, attorneys, and moving companies. Over the years, we've developed a list of *Recommended Vendors* that we update annually; all have been successfully used by either ourselves or our clients. Include an easy to understand collection of frequently asked questions (FAQs) in the materials you give them that will answer most of their common questions. Communicate frequently via e-mail and/or phone calls. Encourage them to ask you questions, lots of them—especially when they catch you speaking "real estate-ese"!

IMMIGRANTS

According to the 2000 Statistical Yearbook of the Immigration and Naturalization Service (INS), the U.S. foreign-born market has grown enormously with more than 16.4 million people entering the United States legally from 1981 to 2000—a figure exceeding the great immigration wave of 1900 to 1914. The U.S. Census Bureau predicts that between 1999 and 2050 the total number of foreign-born will more than double increasing from 26 million to 53.8 million.

During the early years of U.S. residency—less than five years—immigrants are likely to live with other family members or friends. After adapting to their new environment, establishing a stable employment record and income, and building adequate savings, immigrants become avid homebuyers. For many immigrants, homeownership is considered an important milestone in establishing a sense of permanence and belonging in a community. It is an important indicator of social and economic achievement that provides a sense of safety and autonomy.

Specializing in this ever-growing market requires dealing with differences between foreign-born and U.S. buyers. It should be noted that many of these differences also apply to U.S. citizens who are second and even third generation immigrants. According to the NAR's *Expand Your Market* course, there are several key differences:

- Because English is probably a second language, language and terminology barriers are common. Avoid slang; speak clearly. Because real estate itself is a "foreign" language that you speak fluently, explain any terminology you use. If you are using a translator, make sure that he/she is accustomed to dealing with business and real estate terms. If the translator is the "family interpreter," be aware that person may not be the decision maker.
- There are many cultural differences when it comes to physical gestures, contact, and proximity. Avoid "gesture slang" just as you would slang words.
- Business practices you take for granted—negotiating, financing, and buying and selling of property—may be new to a foreign client. For example, Europeans and the Japanese are often unprepared for the roles attorneys may play in U.S. real estate transactions. For specific information about business practices and roles of various professionals, go to the Web site of the International Consortium of Real Estate Associations (ICREA) at *www.WorldProperties.com.*

RELOCATION

This market has changed drastically from the easy days of the of the late '60s and early '70s when companies—sometimes through third-party firms—routinely bought out employees' homes, and the real estate firms selected to list these properties (with no listing referral fee!) enjoyed the best days of relocation. During the '70s and '80s, the cost of relocation rose steadily as a result of significant losses on corporate homes in many troubled markets. Companies spent $50,000 on the average employee transfer and even more in high-cost areas or for international moves, which can exceed a million dollars for a three-year assignment.

New cost-cutting strategies emerged in the '90s. These included a total outsourcing to third-party firms that began attaching referral fees to virtually every transfer connected with their accounts, regardless of whether they had actually placed the referral with the real estate company/sales associate.

In the early 2000s, third-party firms have consolidated, resulting in just a few firms (e.g., Cendant, Prudential, Weichert) controlling the market, and a growing view of relocation services as a commodity rather than an HR function. Referral fees are generally in the 35 percent range, listing fees are often discounted, and real estate firms are being charged annual fees to be eligible for the relocation business. These fees range from $2,500 to as much as $60,000. In addition, participating brokers are required to both attend fee-based special "training" in order to qualify for the business and sign blanket agreements, agreeing to pay referral fees on all employees of that account, whether referred or not.

Even with this commodity approach, the margins of third-party firms have diminished. In an effort to counteract this, they have consolidated offices, cut staff, and tried to replace people with technology. The result has produced service ratings that are at an all-time low.

In spite of this rather bleak picture, the relocation basis is huge. In 2003, there were approximately 600,000 corporate-sponsored moves, of which only 350,000 were part of the formal relocation programs described above, leaving the remaining 275,000 buyers and their families to manage on their own. These latter numbers represent a substantial opportunity for buyer agents and their firms.

Most of the small to medium corporations in every city and town do not have formal relocation programs and yet they do have employees (275,000 of them!) who move and need professional assistance. Develop a list of these companies, make an appointment with the president and offer your services in a "turn-key" package. You and your firm can be their relocation department. Be sure to talk about the challenges facing transferees—cost of living differentials, leaving their roots, difficulty with family assimilation—and your experience in meeting such challenges. Build and then describe your library of resources, including schools, assisted living facilities, international resettlement services, and child care as well as shopping, medical, entertainment, and recreational services.

Whether your relocation client is with a large, medium, or small corporation, all have the same primary need: understanding your market in a relatively short amount of time. Before you meet your client for the first time, send out a relocation package that describes your community and its real estate market. Include sample copies of all the documents he or she will be signing including agency disclosure and/or the buyer agency contract. Communication is key during this time period, not only with the transferee but also with the family. Essentially you'll be doing your buyer counseling session (see Chapter 8) long distance.

When the transferee and family arrive for their initial house-hunting trip, have a welcome basket of maps, local products, and information about yourself and your firm waiting at the hotel/motel. When you meet them, briefly review your state-required agency disclosure and buyer agency contract. Then, take them on a half-day tour of your community's social, cultural, educational, and recreational aspects. Weave in housing in their price range (you've found this out during the pretrip phase) that includes showing the best you have to offer. At the end of this time, in a comfortable location, review what they've learned and their questions. Listen carefully, take notes. Based on this information, design the next day's "serious" house hunting; be prepared to write an offer.

SECOND HOME/RESORT BUYERS

Sales of second homes rose from 264,000 units in 1991 to 359,000 in 2001. According to NAR's chief economist, David Lereah, this accounts for about 6 percent of all homes sales. Overall, the U.S. Census Bureau reported that there were 9.2 million secondary residences in 2002.

A 2002 NAR survey of second-home ownership revealed that 40 percent of those surveyed indicated that it was because of the stock market slump over the past two years that they were considering investing in a second home. At the same time, refinancing has been at an all-time high, often freeing up cash that many have elected to reinvest in real estate that is perceived to be more reliable than the stock market.

Second homes usually fall into two categories: a vacation "home away from home" or a rental property in the college town for the college age children to inhabit while appreciation helps to provide for their education (see Chapter 11 for investment buyers). The vacation home is often located in resort areas such as ski villages, beach towns, or the middle of nowhere.

According to July 2003 information developed by *www.Escape-Homes.com*, the top emerging second-home markets are all relatively small communities characterized by easy access to outdoor activities. The top five are: Burnside, Kentucky; Caribou, Maine; Ely, Minnesota; Island Park, Idaho; and Ketchikan, Arkansas.

These buyers have usually bought before, are sophisticated, and often pay cash. Most rent before purchasing and take time learning the area as they look for convenient access to the reasons they find the area appealing—but when they decide to buy, they want to move quickly. Your biggest challenges are educating these buyers about inventory, pricing, amenities, and what it's like to own versus rent a vacation property. Often the second home must meet multiple needs—a place to gather with family and friends, realize appreciation, and retire. Once they've bought, you'll often need to be their local connection, someone who can find caretakers, potential renters, and maintenance workers. Communication is usually long-distance and best done via e-mail.

FOR-SALE-BY-OWNERS (FSBOS)

In most areas of the country, FSBOs make up approximately 15 percent of the properties on the market at any given time. This percentage usually increases during sellers' markets and decreases during buyers' markets.

For buyers' agents, FSBOs are potential clients: they're unrepresented and they're moving . . . *somewhere*. Finding FSBOs is easy: they put signs with phone numbers in their yards and advertise in the newspaper, in home magazines, and on the Internet. Develop a database that tracks the FSBOs in your area over time. Contact the FSBOs within the first week; continue to communicate weekly if possible.

When contacting the FSBO, tell them you are not looking to list their home. Rather you'd like the opportunity to interview to be their buyer's agent when they are successful in selling their property. Determine whether they plan to stay in the area in which case be prepared with a "Buyer's Handbook" (please see Chapter 8) that is specifically designed for the FSBO. Explain your services and ask for permission to stay in touch with them during their sale process, otherwise behaving as you normally would as a buyer's agent. If they are leaving the area, be prepared to refer them to a colleague in the area to which they are moving.

CREDIT-IMPAIRED BUYERS

Today, many buyers who'd like to be homeowners find that they cannot qualify conventionally or through FHA due to their low credit scores or other circumstances. There are two major ways for buyers' agents to assist such buyers: (1) introduce them to a credit counselor and/or loan officer who will help buyers develop a plan to improve their credit over time or (2) work with the National Home Buyers Assistance (NHBA).

NHBA is a privately held franchisor, headquartered in Denver, with a unique Lease-to-Own program that allows credit-impaired homebuyers to select virtually any home that's for sale in their local markets with minimal restrictions. If you have such a buyer client, have them contact NHBA at (303)703-6422 to find a franchisee in your area. If your buyer applies and is approved, you would then be asked to take the client house shopping for the next 30 days for a home within the client's price range.

When the house is chosen, the NHBA franchisee will act as a "big brother" (investor), stepping in and purchasing the home for your credit-impaired buyer (at which time you'll be paid your commission as in any normal transaction). During the next 12 months, buyers are given time and advice on cleaning up their credit issues, thereby converting themselves (hopefully) into qualified buyers by the end of the year. At this time, the buyer can receive up to 50 percent of their rent back as a credit towards the down payment on what is now "their" home.

NHBA is the brainchild of Michael Shinn, a respected leader in the Colorado real estate community for the past 35 years. He believes there is a political, social, and moral imperative to help credit-impaired Americans achieve home ownership. His goal is to expand to 10,000 franchises across the nation in the next decade. Additional information can be found at his Web site, *www.nhba.com,* or by calling the above number. NHBA's address is 6600 E. Hampden Avenue, Denver, CO 80224.

LUXURY HOME BUYERS

Households that earn at least $100,000 now (2004) represent 14 percent of the population, and the number is expected to hit 17 percent by 2010 according to The Conference Board, a New York-based nonprofit research organization.

As might be expected, most of these buyers are busy professionals with little extra time, and/or members of "old money families." They expect to be catered to and are often quite picky and want just the "right" house. They might buy on a moment's notice—or they may wait 10 years. Your biggest challenges are: (1) educating many buyers that the money they have may not buy all the amenities they want in a specific location and (2) dealing with fickleness because most transactions aren't need-based. Your communications should be brief e-mails or voice mail messages that get right to the point. You'll find that luxury buyers typically trust the professionals they hire to do the job in the same way they expect to be trusted.

These buyers are often most comfortable with buyers' agents who travel in their circles. Their expectations differ from those of buyers of lower-priced homes. They expect you to understand what they mean when they say they want a gourmet kitchen or a spa bathroom, and they rarely mean a fixer-upper that could be converted into a luxury home. Turn-key is definitely best. Many buyers in this market insist on privacy and security, which may mean a suburban gated community or a high-rise with a doorman.

In 2003, well-known author and speaker Laurie Moore-Moore founded the Institute for Luxury Home Marketing, an industrywide training and certification program focused on the upper-tier residential market. Its designation is the Certified Luxury Home Marketing Specialist (CLHMS). Upper-tier is defined as properties that fall within the top 10 percent of an MLS area's annual home sales, but never less than

$500,000. For additional information, the Institute can be contacted at (214) 485-3000 or *www.luxuryhomemarketing.com.*

SENIORS

According to the U.S. Department of Health and Human Services, there will be about 71.5 million Americans over age 65 by 2030, a huge percentage of the total expected 2030 population. Most of this population growth is because baby boomers begin to reach age 65 in 2011.

Seniors have often lived in their current residence for decades and are hesitant to relocate; moving is often a very difficult transition. As a result, building a strong relationship-based on trust is more important when working with seniors than with any other group. This may take six months to a year. They want compassion and patience. In other words, you are counseling as well as selling. Remember, seniors come from an era where service was expected and automatic; their word was their bond and loyalty and honesty were the norm. According to Jill Corliss, cofounder of the Senior Advantage Real Estate Council (SAREC), "Never lie and always keep your word, even in small things, such as returned phone calls. And always be on time for your appointments."

Unless you're a qualified financial planner, do not offer specific financial advice; instead partner with a CFP. Seniors are usually on fixed incomes and therefore do not want or cannot afford to add debt in order to buy the replacement home.

According to a 2003 study by the National Association of Home Builders, seniors (age 50 and above) want low maintenance, a location closer to the children, central air conditioning, lever handle/doorknobs, full bath on the entry level, and an attached garage. The results of the study showed that: (1) 75 percent of seniors purchased one-story homes; (2) 60 percent avoided mortgage hassles by paying cash; (3) those who did finance preferred 15-year mortgages; and (4) only 10 percent elected adjustable-rate financing.

Communicating with seniors is best done directly, face to face, rather than by e-mail. They'll generally expect you to come to their home rather than have them come to your office. Your older clients may not always remember what you discussed at your last meeting, so confirmation in writing is always a good idea that can save face for both you and your client. Many seniors have grown children who want to be involved in the decision making, however, unless the parents are ill, this is okay only if you have permission from their parents, your senior clients.

Specialized training in working with seniors can be obtained by taking the SAREC's Seniors Real Estate Specialist (SRES) designation course. The designation was acquired by a subsidiary of the California Association of REALTORS® and is formally recognized by NAR. SAREC can be reached at (800) 500-4564.

BABY BOOMERS

Those born between 1946 and 1964 are generally lumped into the cohort of the U.S. population tagged baby boomers, a group of about 77.7 million that currently make up about 27.5 percent of the total population. By 2006, the oldest of this group will become 60, an age that begins to seriously look at retirement.

In general, baby boomers grew up in a nurturing environment in which mom stayed at home and dad worked. They
experienced the post-World War II economic boom and were
the first generation of American women who, in large numbers, made money and weren't afraid to spend it. They're optimistic workaholics who are relying on Social Security, a
pension, and personal savings for retirement while counting
on the same level of Medicare coverage as their parents now
enjoy. They appreciate democracy and teamwork. In the 2000
presidential election, approximately 59 percent of baby
boomers voted.

Baby boomers have a higher level of education than any
generation before them—88.8 percent have completed high
school and 28.5 percent have a bachelor's degree or more.
Thanks to this increased educational attainment and work-
place achievement (especially among women), boomers will
have more cash to spend in their retirement years.

Boomers today make up nearly 60 percent of all divorced
people over the age of 15 in the United States, although they
account for just 40 percent of the population age 15 and older.
The percentage of boomers who never married (12.6 percent)
is significantly higher than prior generations: 5.2 percent of
those 55–64; 3.9 percent of those 65 and older. According to
U.S. Census data, nearly a third of boomers are single, compared with just 12 percent of today's seniors. This means that
more boomers are living on their own and will be as the oldest
of them draw their first Social Security checks in 2008.

But their expectations for housing will not get smaller
according to a 2004 Del Web Group survey that concludes that
single boomers will not scale down their shelter requirements
as they enter retirement and will be "just as likely to buy an

average size two- or three-bedroom home," using the extra room for home offices or exercise rooms. Of the baby boomers with children, this same study found that about 36 percent plan to move into a new home when they become empty nesters. Of these who plan to move, about 36 percent said they will move more than three hours away from their current home. About 44 percent said the top reason for leaving their current home is to move into a smaller home, and 44 percent said they want a home that requires less maintenance.

The Webb study also found that about 24 percent of baby boomers anticipate that parents or in-laws would move in with them and about one-quarter of the survey respondents said they expect their children to move back in with them (and 28 percent of them plan to charge their children rent!). Many of today's baby boomers are far from the typical real estate client as many are experiencing the unique situation of becoming caregivers to their parents while raising children and planning for their own retirement.

According to a 2001 survey commissioned by the GE Center for Financial Learning, 70 percent of boomers, unlike their parents, are not relying on their families to take care of their long-term needs in their later years. Instead, they'll hire help. But, according to William Serow, director of the Center for Study of Population at Florida State University, because of living healthier lifestyles than their parents and grandparents and because of advances in medical technology, boomers likely won't demand help from the private sector on a regular basis until the 2020s.

Boomers are optimistic about old age with nearly half looking forward to their retirement years. According to the GE Center for Financial Learning study "Secure Tomorrow's

Autonomy Today," a majority of boomers don't believe that aging will impair their abilities in any way: 55 percent believe that they will still be able to perform basic tasks independently when they reach their 80s.

Part of the boomers' optimism may be based on expected or received inheritance. The boomers' parents, who are getting older and frailer, vividly remember the Depression and have held onto their homes as long as possible. Some are now moving into nursing care and either selling their homes or giving them to their boomer children. Based on an earlier Cornell University study, this will represent a $10 trillion wealth transfer into the hands of the baby boomers. Researchers expect this money will be used for college education of boomer children and/or put toward a second home.

Thus, for buyers' agents of any age, the baby boom generation represents opportunities for selling both replacement homes (in 1998, the homeownership rate for boomers was 70.5 percent) and second homes. This is especially true if you live and work in one of the nine states where over 50 percent of all baby boomers live: California, Texas, New York, Florida, Pennsylvania, Illinois, Ohio, Michigan, and New Jersey.

GEN XERS

Born between 1965 and 1982, Generation X, the 50 million "latch key kids" who came home from elementary school, took the door key from its hiding place, let themselves in, and then had to fend for themselves, are very different from their baby boom parents. They've grown up in an environment in which computers were as common as telephones and refrigerators were to their parents and are the first generation to be completely computer literate. They shop (do research on) the Internet for everything, and when they narrow their choices down to two or three, they arrive at the office/dealer/store ready to make a fast decision; this includes buying a home. During the process they typically gather and share input with a wider range and number of acquaintances than older generations.

According to a recent (2002) study done for *Builder Magazine*, half of the Gen Xers already own their own homes and most became homeowners shortly after finishing their education. Many buy homes earlier than prior generations because they have a higher proportion of two-income households. However, often Gen Xers get a jump-start from their better-heeled parents, experiencing wealth transfers long before estates and inheritance taxes are part of the discussion.

Bruce Tulgan, author of *Winning the Talent Wars* and president of Rainmaker Thinking, a research firm that studies the work habits of Gen Xers, says this is a generation that doesn't want to be "sold." "You've got to be straight with them. They are the most media-savvy generation in history," he says. They are fiercely independent, very serious about work, and use the Web for the flexibility and resources it offers.

In terms of housing preferences, formal living and dining rooms don't make sense. Highest on their list of priorities, according to the *Builder Magazine* survey, are abundant counter space in their kitchens, lots of storage and closet space, good energy efficiency (with passive solar designs), high-speed Web access, and a large yard. The first question they're likely to ask is "What is the high-speed data provider at this location?" and you'd better have the answer. They want the ability to work from their homes so look for homes with desk areas with all the lines cable-ready and modems readily available.

Gen Xers are menu-driven, preferring to be given choices from the general to the specific in everything, just like a Web page's drop-down menu. They're often referred to as maximizers: they want the most for their time, money, and experience, as well as the space in their homes. They're all about innovation, speed, and themselves, living in the present, experimenting with what's possible, and looking for immediate results.

Their families take extreme priority; instead of trying to fit family into their work life as the baby boomers do, Gen-X parents are more likely to fit work into their family life. Twenty-five percent of Gen-X moms spend 12 hours a day or more on child-raising and household tasks and 48 percent of Gen-X dads say they spend three to six hours daily on those activities.

But this family-first, career-second approach appears to carry a financial penalty according to James Chung who ran the study for Reach Advisors. Gen Xers' housing debt is 62 percent higher than it was for boomers at the same age, and according to the U.S. General Accounting Office, Gen Xers' total debt levels are a staggering 78 percent higher than was the case for boomers at a comparable age. Fortunately, Gen Xers are relatively frugal having a lean lifestyle, buying what they need, but having the will power to not always buy what they want.

In terms of both recreation and work, Gen Xers prefer to do things "alone together." They like working parallel with others, doing their part, but they generally don't want to be responsible for the whole project. They're highly independent yet desire personal interaction and constant feedback. Change is comfortable and Gen Xers expect change.

For most buyers' agents, this means changing your approach and work habits. The Gen Xers want Web sites that are fast, easy to navigate, and have a lot of information. They want instant response and want it live. So, shorten up your presentations, but make them crystal clear. Take the time to explain the process completely, but keep it simple and straightforward—eliminate the fluff. Once they understand the process, Gen Xers are going to ask what they can do to save time and money. Be prepared! Ask them to help in finding the right property through their use of the Internet; let them contribute and be your partner.

At the same time, assert your expertise—that body of knowledge you've accumulated with experience as well as the initials after your name that are recognized within the industry for your skills and insights. But don't be surprised if your Gen-Xer clients question authority and "this is the way it's always been done" statements. Many Gen Xers may treat the sales process as a game, asking pointed questions to watch the agent squirm. Just remember, it never hurts to ask and watch what happens. As Bonnie Sparks, influential author and trainer, says, "The fastest way to win their (Gen Xers') loyalty is to seek out and value their opinions, to respect their intelligence . . . and most of all . . . to treat them like the adults they are."

SUMMARY

Buyers' agents have a multitude of market segments in which to specialize. Each can provide an excellent source of clients and therefore income, but not without spending time and effort in developing market expertise. These segments include the following buyers: first-time, immigrants, relocation, second-home/resort, FSBOs, credit-impaired, luxury, and the largest of today's demographic groups: seniors, baby boomers, and Gen Xers. Successful buyers' agents select one or more of these segments to "farm."

REVIEW QUESTIONS

1. Which of the following is not a market for buyers' agents?
   a. Seniors
   b. Credit-impaired buyers
   c. Other agents' buyers
   d. Second-home buyers

ANSWER:

c. There are many demographic and geographic niches a buyer's agent can develop. However, under no circumstances should a buyer's agent "farm" other agents' buyers.

2. Baby boomers were born between
   a. 1900 and 1924.
   b. 1965 and 1982.
   c. 1983 and 2000.
   d. 1946 and 1964.

ANSWER:

d. Answer (b) is the dates for Gen Xers; (a) and (c) are made up dates.

3. Which of the following best relates to corporate relocation?

a. Has changed from an HR function to a commodity controlled by a few large companies

b. Is a good source of buyers for whom no referral fees are charged

c. Resulted in more than one million corporate-sponsored moves in 2003

d. Requires no special skills for the buyer's agent

ANSWER:

a. Unlike the earlier years of corporate relocation, this HR function is now recognized as a major source of income and, as a result, has become a commodity controlled largely by Cendant, Prudential, and Weichert. Referral fees are substantial, usually between 30 percent and 40 percent. There were approximately 600,000 corporate moves in 2003. Handling buyers being relocated by their company requires special skills.

4. Which of the following best relates to for-sale-by owners?

a. Make up approximately 15 percent of the properties on the market at any given time

b. Can be effectively "farmed" by buyers' agents

c. Are easy to find

d. All of the above

ANSWER:

d. FSBOs can be farmed effectively by developing a database from ads that are easy to find on the Internet, in specialized magazines, and in newspapers. The FSBO market averages about 15 percent nationally; this percentage usually goes up in strong sellers' markets and down in strong buyers' markets.

CHAPTER 7

Prospecting for Buyer Clients

Prospecting must be done continually, as results certainly don't happen overnight. A 2004 research project commissioned by HouseValues, Inc. found that buyers began thinking that they should buy a home up to four years before actually doing so. A motivating factor such as wanting/needing a larger home, financial advantages of buying instead of renting, family reasons, and job relocation had to happen before buyers began the homebuying process.

HouseValues' research found that on average, the homebuying process itself took 16.4 months, split into three phases:

1. Thinking about buying—7.1 months
2. Researching a purchase—5.3 months
3. Actively looking for a home—4.1 months.

"Interesting," you say, "but how did they choose an agent?" The results were a real eye-opener. 61.8 percent of the buyers selected their agent in just one to three days.

Based on this study, the key to your success is forming long-term relationships with as many prospective buyers as possible, as early as possible in the process. This chapter will look at numerous methods of doing just this, including advertising, use of the Internet, referrals, farming, and homebuyer seminars.

ADVERTISING

As with any effective advertising, the keys to promoting yourself as a buyer's agent are simplicity, consistency, and adequate coverage.

Simplicity

Simplicity is perhaps the most difficult of the three characteristics to ensure, because the terminology of real estate is very like a foreign language to most people and therefore requires explanations that are rarely simple. Avoid such terms as *single agency,* because that begs for an explanation of the alternatives (dual agency and no agency). Even *buyer agency* is not sufficiently simple; it may prompt a request for an explanation of the legal concept of agency, which many agents themselves do not understand. Instead, use simple terms such as *buyer's agent, buyer's broker,* and *buyer's representative.* Most people readily comprehend that such an agent, broker, or representative must surely be working *for* the buyer.

If the advertising medium chosen allows the luxury of description, keep it simple by using phrases such as

- "Let us work *for you:* we're buyers' agents."
- "We'll work to get you the best price and terms: we represent buyers."
- "Attention buyers: as buyers' brokers, we'll take care of you."

The proper time for detailed explanations of the benefits of buyer agency is during the counseling appointment (see Chapter 8); advertising explanations are designed to grab attention and bring in those phone or e-mail responses!

Consistency

The second characteristic, *consistency,* means that your message is always basically the same. For example, the three sample descriptions above all revolve around one theme: that buyers' agents take care of their buyer clients, working to get them the best price and the best terms.

When designing your advertising campaign to introduce your services as a buyer's agent, review your agency policy, your goals and objectives, your practice, and your philosophy. Then select the basic theme apparent in all of them. To obtain consistency, that theme must be expressed in each ad, whether it be in print; on the radio, television, or Internet; or in presentations to the public.

This consistency can be achieved either simply or in a more sophisticated manner. Simple, and sometimes subtle, methods include a logo and/or quoted line that is present in every ad you and your company run. More sophisticated methods include excerpts from interviews with satisfied clients and associates that reflect your basic theme.

Adequate Coverage

The third key to effective advertising, *adequate coverage,* is usually the most difficult because, with the exception of the Internet, it is the most expensive. Once designed, your simple, consistent theme must appear sufficiently often in enough different media forms to cause your public to call on you and your company when they begin to consider buying real estate.

In addition to normal print advertising, consider doing an "advertorial"—an ad that's intended to look like an article. Curtis Hall, associate broker with RE/MAX Anasazi Realty in Tempe, Arizona, says his single best promotion was a two-page, full-color advertorial in a city magazine. It touted his accomplishments and the benefits of buyer agency. That ad "catapulted my career into orbit," says Hall. "It was the best $2,000 I ever spent."

When Paul Sutherland was a buyer's agent with RE/MAX Affiliates in Alexandria, Virginia, promotional nirvana came in the form of a TV spot on a cable channel. As potential buyers watched the endless string of listings on the all real estate network, Sutherland's ad popped up and asked, "You're not represented? What are you waiting for?" "After that ad started running, the phone rang off the hook," says Sutherland, now president of Paul Sutherland's Success Seminars, based in Sarasota Springs, Florida.

Different types of buyers can be reached through different media. Reach first-time buyers through homebuying seminars, direct mailings, print advertising, and your Web site. Reach seniors and/or their grown children through Web sites, ads in local, often free newspapers geared to seniors. Reach resort buyers with Web sites featuring virtual tours and detailed information on room layouts, view, prices, taxes, condo fees, and area amenities. Reach luxury buyers through high-quality brochures with color photographs and floor plans; Web sites with virtual tours; ads in upscale publications; professional newsletters; digital photos; special-interest groups, such as alumni associations; and social networks. Reach corporate relocation staff by sending letters, flyers, and postcards to human resource managers and placing ads in annual relocation directories and periodicals.

All of the markets described in Chapter 6 are niches, smaller segments of the larger market. Determining a niche you want to focus on and then finding effective and efficient ways of reaching that niche is your key to success. Instead, most agents waste hundreds if not thousands of dollars each year on generic ads and bulk mail that doesn't speak to anyone in particular. One effective solution that we've found is a book written by Martha Woodbury, a former experienced REALTOR®, called *The Prospect Generator-Profit Generating Workbook–7 Steps to Building a Better Niche for Real Estate Agents.* You can choose any one of four niches: first-time buyers, move-up buyers, empty nesters, or home-officed entrepreneurs. *The Prospect Generator* then provides personalized, emotional, direct-response classified and small display ads; sequenced follow-up letters, voice mail, or answering machine scripts; direct response follow-up post cards; and questionnaires and surveys. You can download this in PDF for under $35 or purchase a printed full system for $179. Check this out at *www.niches-works.com.*

Before placing your ads, arrange for the prospective news-papers, magazines, yellow page directories, and radio and tele-vision stations to furnish you with data regarding the number of people they reach and the demographics of their audiences. Study these materials in light of both cost and your goals before making an ad-buying decision.

If the cost is simply too high (or even if it is not but you want additional coverage), research your own sources of buyer clients. Although some may be from responses to ads and signs, most will probably be from people that you know either directly or indirectly. Analyze those sources and design means of communicating your buyer agency services to them. These means may include distribution of business cards and personal brochures, scheduled phone calls, personal letters, presenta-tions to service clubs, or support for your favorite charity made in the name of your company. The list is limited only by your creativity and desire for outreach. Remember that many of these means of communication do not require substantial dollars, but they well may require considerable time.

Advertising on the Internet is fairly inexpensive. Securing a domain name/URL address is about $100 with monthly main-tenance costs of $30 to $50 for 25 mb. The major expense is Web site design, which varies widely. Effective Internet adver-tising follows the same rules of simplicity and consistency dis-cussed above. Its results, however, can be excellent because the average Web user generally has a high income and therefore purchases more expensive property.

It is easy to determine whether your coverage is adequate. If you have enough business to satisfy your needs and wants, to meet your goals, then your coverage is adequate! If you do not have enough, then your coverage is inadequate. You need to do either more advertising or more personal communicating, or both, the keys always being simplicity and consistency. Like most truths, this is a very simplistic concept, but one that will pay off handsomely if you implement it with discipline.

THE INTERNET

The California Association of REALTORS®' (CAR) 2004 *Internet Versus Traditional Buyer Study* found that buyers using the Internet climbed to 56 percent, a steady rise from the 28 percent CAR found in 2000. This number is expected to continue to climb as younger buyers enter the market.

CAR's study showed that Internet buyers spend more than twice as much time (5.9 weeks) as traditional buyers (2.1 weeks) on research before contacting an agent—and once Internet buyers begin working with agents, they spend less time (1.9 weeks as compared to 7.1 weeks) looking and tour fewer homes (6.1 homes versus 15.4 homes). While Internet buyers considered online information to be valuable, they ultimately turned to REALTORS® both for their interpretation of that information and for their expertise and judgment throughout the homebuying process. These buyers tended to view their relationship with their agent as a partnership and looked for speed, efficiency, and timely communications.

These Internet respondents were younger, with a mean age of 38.5 years, compared to 43.5 for traditional buyers. Twenty-three percent reported that they were first-time buyers compared to 7 percent of traditional buyers.

During their research phase, Internet buyers often make inquiries about specific homes but, according to Allan Dalton, *REALTOR.com* president, in a 2004 interview, most (fully 70 percent) inquiries do not receive a response or the response is very tardy. However, for agents who respond immediately, the conversion rate is tremendous—about 20 percent—*REALTOR.com* data show. The rate is only about 2 percent for those who don't respond immediately. One out of every six unique visitors to *REALTOR.com* sends an e-mail (1 million e-mail messages/month) to a real estate practitioner and two out of every six call a practitioner.

Given this horrible response data, agents must develop a procedure that is both timely and helpful. The Kleimer Company in the Vail Valley, Avon, Colorado, has a very effective system for handling every type of e-mailed request. Their theme is a soft but strong "I want to help you" message. Here's what they do:

- Each lead goes first to the owner-broker who then forwards it on to an agent based on their farm area.
- The agent responds as soon as possible—no later than 24 hours—saying, "Thank you for visiting our Web site. How can we help?"
- If a phone number is available, the agent calls at least twice initially to tell the prospect about the agency's "buyer instant notification program." Offered through the MLS, this allows Web site visitors to log information

about the kind of home they would like, including number of bedrooms, price range, area, and so on. The prospect then receives automatic e-mail responses each time new MLS listings come up that match the specifications.

- If there is no answer to the phone call, the agent leaves a message about the program and e-mails a thank-you note if the call is not returned.

- If the prospect answers the phone, the agent explains the buyer instant-notification program and offers to mail out a buyer's packet.

- If the prospect seems interested in moving forward with buying a home, the agent uses a standard form to gather contact information and details about the prospect's needs

This call to the e-customer is important, because it's your first opportunity to build a relationship. Using a form prevents you from forgetting anything and provides material to keep the conversation flowing.

Bottom line, the Internet is an incredible source of buyer clients that most agents simply do not use effectively. Don't be part of the majority: commit to implementing a procedure of immediate and helpful response.

FARMING

Farming can be defined as activities designed to establish a long-term relationship with a group of people. It can be either geographic or social in character.

An effective geographic farming method for buyers' agents is consistent contacts in a geographic area inhabited by people who are likely buyers. Apartment complexes, especially those that cater to young professionals and families with incomes adequate to qualify for a home mortgage, are obvious candidates. Be aware, however, that many such complexes prohibit door-to-door solicitation. Mailing personal letters to tenants is often the best alternative, especially if it is followed up with a phone call. In most metropolitan areas, a listing of the names, addresses, and telephone numbers for the occupants can easily be obtained from a city directory; the most common of these directories is published by Polk.

Social farming requires a long-term commitment, but usually yields excellent results. *Social farming* means being an active participant in a club, business group, school, church, or other organization. To be effective, your membership cannot be perceived by the other members as simply another of your prospecting tools. You must be a member because you believe in the organization; you must be a participant because you believe you can make a difference. Over time, you will gain the respect and trust of the organization and its members. Because they know that you are a real estate agent, that respect and trust will eventually be expressed in the form of client relationships.

Perhaps the most important key to effective social farming is to avoid individual business discussions with other members while participating in the organization. Should a member ask you for advice, attempt to schedule a phone call or meeting outside the organization. If someone wants to begin a simple discussion about real estate, after a pleasant, short answer, politely change the subject to matters pertinent to the organization. Such precautions will go a long way toward preventing another member who casually overhears your conversation from assuming that you are merely using your membership as a source of business and from spreading harmful gossip to that effect.

Thus, active membership in any organization may be an excellent source of clients, but only if you are a member first because of your belief in the value of the organization. Unfortunately, the motives of salespeople are always suspect in the minds of many, and only your actual behavior can remove or at least minimize such suspicions.

Farming corporate personnel managers can be most effective, given the multiplying effect. As mentioned in Chapter 6, corporations engaged in relocating employees are especially concerned about the employee's happiness and the employee's not overpaying for a house that may later be owned and sold by the corporation during the next relocation. Point out that hiring/recommending buyer agency services can be advantageous for a corporation.

REFERRALS AND REPEAT BUSINESS

Referrals and repeat business are always the best sources of business because prospective clients come with either a recommendation regarding the quality of your services from a trusted acquaintance or a memory of superior service. As a result, you spend less time selling the value of your service and more time actually providing service.

Referrals and repeat business, however, must be cultivated through periodic reminders that you are still active in business and concerned about your clients' welfare and happiness. This can most easily be accomplished by contacting every past client and past referral source on a quarterly basis. At a minimum, one of these contracts should be in person or by phone, the others can be by personal letter, greeting card, flyer, or newsletter. The effectiveness of such contacts is substantially increased by the degree to which they are personal: a visit is better than a phone call; a personal note is better than a flyer; a newsletter with a personal note written across its face is better than the newsletter alone.

Two techniques that increase the effectiveness of such contacts are (1) saying "thank you" for past business and (2) mentioning that your success depends on referrals and repeat business and asking your contacts if they know of anyone currently interested in purchasing real estate. For a variety of reasons, most people feel good when they help someone else, especially if it is someone (you) whom they like and trust. Make it your goal to give them the opportunity to feel good!

Few agents ask for referrals frequently enough, usually from fear of rejection. You'll find it easier if, rather than thinking of the request for a business referral as an event, you consider it a process. The following is a four-step procedure developed by Stephen Canale, a highly respected speaker, trainer, and author:

1. First, plant the seed. In your next buyer counseling session (see Chapter 8), make sure you emphasize that you prefer to do business on a referral basis. If the prospect has come to you through a referral of some kind, then reinforce that the reason you're willing to work with them is because of the referral from the mutual acquaintance. If the customer came to you from some other source, an

incoming call for instance, then point out your willingness to work with them as a special exception.

2. The second step is to obtain a commitment for a future event. Say something like "If I agree to go to work for you now, and can successfully handle this transaction to your satisfaction, would you be willing to refer business to me in the future?" There's no pressure or immediate need to act and their obligation is contingent upon your doing a good job for them, which of course is something they want.

3. Step three is reinforcement. When your immediate business with the client is complete, remind them of their agreement to refer business to you whenever the opportunity arises. Say, "It's been a pleasure working with you and I hope we can work together again in the future. By the way, when you know of someone who needs to buy or sell, after giving out my name and number, please call or e-mail me directly to let me know that you've referred them. As I told you when we first met, I generally only work on a referral basis, and I'd hate to have your friends leave me a message and not realize that they were referred by you. If you can let me know to expect their call ahead of time, I would appreciate it. And, I'll make sure I do my very best for them."

4. The final step is positive reinforcement. Reward the referral action by (a) immediately thanking the person who sent you the referral, while reaffirming that you'll provide the best possible service to the friend, neighbor, or relative; (b) keeping the person who sent the referral apprised of the status as much as is appropriate, such as when the transaction has been

successfully closed; and (c) sending a personal gift, gift certificate, or gift basket with a handwritten "thank you" card. Take every opportunity to again remind the referrer of how much you appreciate his or her efforts on your behalf.

A special set of people that you should cultivate as sources of referrals is composed of other professionals: lawyer, accountant, banker, doctor, financial planner, and anyone else who provides you with professional-level services. Recommendations from these sources carry great weight for many people and are thus more likely to be followed. Most of these professionals act as fiduciaries and place a high value on your ability to represent the referees (often their own clients) they send to you. Remember, too, that not only are these professionals excellent referral sources but also they themselves are potential buyer clients!

Annual client appreciation events, although major undertakings, are one of the most effective ways of staying in touch with your referral base.

PUBLIC SEMINARS

Giving a public seminar on any topic related to buyer agency or buying real estate allows you to demonstrate your expertise to a group of people otherwise unknown to you. The audience for such seminars can vary from service clubs to small groups who attend because of a personal invitation, to classes of students willing to pay tuition to learn from you, to large audiences made up of people who were attracted by newspaper, radio, or television advertising. Each type of seminar has its own problems, logistics, and costs that you must consider before initiating it.

In addition to the above considerations, you should honestly analyze your speaking abilities, which may vary relative to audience size. If you feel inadequate, look at the possibility of sponsoring a gifted and knowledgeable speaker. Hire the speaker both to teach effectively the concepts you feel are important and to "carry the company flag" by encouraging members of the audience to use the buyer agency services that you and your company offer.

SUMMARY

Prospecting for buyer clients requires careful planning if you are to use your available resources most efficiently. These resources include not only your financial ability but also your personal time. A great deal of personal discipline aided by a readily accessible database can yield a steadily increasing business.

The best sources of buyer clients include advertising, farming, referrals, and public seminars. Before deciding on which prospecting methods best fit you and your company, analyze the cost and effectiveness of each source.

REVIEW QUESTIONS

1. Effective advertising is
   a. simple.
   b. complex.
   c. full of terminology.
   d. based on many changing messages.

ANSWER:

   a. Advertising that is complex, full of terminology, and frequently changes its message is ineffective. The best advertising is simple because it can be remembered.

2. Niche markets
   a. require specialization.
   b. require databases to effectively market.
   c. can be reached most effectively via generic ads that are bulk mailed.
   d. Both (a) and (b)

ANSWER:

   d. Niche markets cannot be developed by generic ads that are bulk mailed. To effectively develop a niche market requires specialization (knowledge, contract clauses, demographics, etc.) and a good database.

3. Internet buyers
   a. make up more than 50 percent of all buyers.
   b. spend twice as much time on research than traditional buyers.
   c. spend less time looking at houses with agents than do traditional buyers.
   d. All of the above

ANSWER:

d. Internet buyers are rapidly becoming a significant part (56 percent in 2004 in a California survey) of the market. Because of the large amount of research done by these buyers, they spend less time actually looking at property.

8

The Buyer Counseling Session

The critical element of every successful buyer client relationship is the initial counseling session, during which the agent and principal discuss and thoroughly understand each other's expectations and their proposed agency relationship. The agent asks probing questions to understand the client's wants and needs and describes the events that will occur during the transaction and their probable timing. Such professional counseling should occur before any significant action related to the transaction takes place. Without question, this should happen before the first property is presented.

Buyer counseling sessions are usually fairly lengthy, because a wide range of topics must be understood. The topics include building rapport, presenting the buyer's handbook, determining probable events and timing, explaining disclosure and the agency representation decision, training the buyer client, determining wants and needs, and financial qualifying. Our experience is that, at a minimum, one hour is required for the meeting, which should occur in a private office setting free from interruptions. In general, buyers find such sessions very valuable: a 2004 survey conducted for Land-American Financial Group reported that 86 percent of home-buyers found the buying process difficult and perplexing. Your job is to make the process rational and understandable.

Organization of this detail is best done with a buyer's handbook, a professional tool that will give you an edge over your competitors. As is true of anything used to enhance your business image, the appearance and presentation of your book must be polished. Pages should be uniform, printed, and possibly enclosed in plastic inserts. Use graphics and include sample documents. If you use a PowerPoint presentation, be sure to provide the buyer with a printed three-to-a-page handout. In any case, tell the buyer, "this is yours to keep; feel free to take notes as we proceed."

Guide the buyer through the book page by page, detailing the benefits and features of the information. During this initial inteview with a client, listening is your most crucial selling skill. When asking questions, 20 percent of your time should be speaking and 80 percent concentrating on what the client is saying, giving them feedback, and making every effort to see their point of view. Clients tell us that our best real estate agents are not the best talkers—they are the best listeners.

Components of your buyer's handbook are noted in the sections that follow.

BUILDING RAPPORT AND TRUST

Although the building of rapport and trust is one of the skills that separates top producers from the remainder, several aspects other than personality can be defined, practiced, and learned. In addition to the specific suggestions that follow, remember that the building of rapport continues throughout your relationship with the buyer and that, once built, your client's trust can easily be destroyed by a dishonest or disloyal word or act.

Early in the counseling appointment, present your qualifications to the prospective buyer clients. These qualifications should include a résumé of both your experience (or your company's if you are recently licensed) and any special education or training applicable to the practice of buyer agency and real estate in general.

In presenting your experience, include years of practice, number of transactions, and/or transaction dollar volume on both an annual and averaged basis. People want to know that they are working with a successful, experienced agent. However, even more important than past success and experience are honesty and enthusiasm, two characteristics available to even the novice agent. If you are inexperienced, talk enthusiastically about the experience and good reputation of your broker and your company.

Special training and education, especially when it has been formalized by a designation such as the National Association of REALTORS®' Accredited Buyer Representataive (ABR), Certified Residential Specialist (CRS), Certified International Property Specialist (CIPS), Certified Commercial Investment Member (CCIM), and Certified Real Estate Brokerage Manager (CRB), should be described briefly to the prospective clients. Participation in courses and seminars will enhance your reputation as a real estate expert.

In addition to your experience and special training describe applicable rules and regulations to which you must

adhere as a licensed agent. REALTORS® should include and discuss the NAR Code of Ethics.

The initial pages of your buyer's handbook should include
a summary of the points just described. The emphasis should
be on clarity and simplicity, as in all the pages that follow.
Remember, your goal is to establish credibility, rapport, and
trust.

THE BUYER'S HANDBOOK

The buyer's handbook describes the details of the homebuying process and includes sample contracts, information on
financing, title insurance, inspections, surveys, appraisals, and
the community. This handbook, when reviewed during the
counseling session, serves to prepare buyers for the transaction details that will occur. Refer to the handbook often as you
proceed through the actual transaction; you will find that buyers' prior contact with this information will result in greater
comfort and understanding when they are actually used.

At a minimum, the buyer's handbook should include the
following information plus any other specifics about your market. Sample contracts, brochures, maps, disclosure information, and so on, should be added in protective plastic sleeves.

A CD of the Buyer's Handbook used by the authors can be
purchased for $19.95; the CD is writable if your computer has
a CD burner; otherwise it is Read Only.

Community Information

Some of the items that should be included and discussed in this section are:

- maps;
- school locations, descriptions, and national test scores; demographic and economic data, including major employers and average cost-of-living details;
- descriptions of parks and other recreational and cultural facilities; and
- location of shopping and transportation.

In larger communities, most of this information can be obtained preprinted from the Chamber of Commerce or the Economic Development Council. The amount of information you present should vary with the buyers' familiarity with the community.

Standard Documents

These materials should include

- sample copies of the purchase and sale agreement (actual documents with all identifying data removed);
- FNMA/FHLMC and/or FHA and/or VA notes and deeds of trust;
- buyer agency contract;
- sample copies of settlement statements; and
- sample title information (e.g., title commitment).

These documents should be clearly identified but not reviewed in detail; request that the buyers read them, with the exception of the buyer agency contract, at their leisure and note any questions, which you will discuss at your next meeting. Tell the buyers that you have excepted the buyer agency contract because you want to review it with them in detail later in the counseling session.

Financing Information

These items can include

- a glossary of financing terminology;
- a blank copy of the FNMA/FHLMC loan application form;
- a list of loan officers and companies that you can highly recommend; and
- a descriptive list of alternative loan types.

Describe the loan process, emphasizing the constant changes in interest rates and points, the probable range of difference among rates offered by lenders on any given day, and the importance of using a lender of good experience and reputation. Tell buyers that the actual loan qualifying process will be done as part of the loan application, but that you will estimate their qualifications later in the counseling session.

The scope of possible approaches to a mortgage in today's market is staggering for both you and your client. Educate them about basic terminology such as *discount points, origination points, closing costs,* and *locking in;* discuss the basic factors that affect interest rates. Perhaps the broadest distinction for which your buyers will require explanation is the differences between fixed rate and variable rate mortgages. For first-time buyers and lower-income buyers you'll also want to describe some of the zero and low down payment, interest only, and numerous municipal and state programs. There are so many plans that even experienced buyers' agents can and do become confused. Bottom line, you should develop a stable of lenders, each of whom specializes in a different area of mortgage lending and then refer your buyers to the appropriate loan officer.

Since many buyers have already contacted a lender, ask if they have. If so, ask them to have their lender provide you with a preapproval letter stating the amount for which they qualify. Should you not be familiar with their lender, call him/her and introduce yourself as you'll need to work closely together.

During the counseling session, use your ability to estimate the buyer's financial qualifications; this is one of your critical skills as a buyer's agent. The emphasis here is on *estimate,* as formal qualifying should, of course, be done by the buyer's lender or other financing professional, whether the purchase is based on cash, commercial mortgage, or owner-carried or other private financing. From a liability standpoint, the real estate licensee should not take on the responsibility of determining for others that the buyer is qualified to fulfill the contract's financial terms.

However, roughly estimating a buyer's qualifications is necessary so that you can determine the price range of the properties you will show. For buyer clients, the upper limit of this range is equal to the loan amount for which they can qualify plus their cash down payment plus the average differential between list and sales price in your market. (For buyer customers, a seller's agent or nonagent should *not* add in this "average differential.")

The process of qualifying is straightforward and, for most loans, is based on two ratios that are applied to the buyer's gross, or before-tax, income. These two ratios are (1) monthly housing expense, usually principal, interest, taxes, insurance (PITI), and homeowner's association fee, if any, divided by gross monthly income and (2) monthly long-term (usually six months or longer) debt including PITI divided by gross monthly income.

The maximum allowable for each ratio varies with the loan type. Generally, these ratios are lower for conventional mortgages and higher for government-insured (FHA) or guaranteed (VA) mortgages and other subsidized loans (such as local bond programs) designed to assist families with low and moderate incomes in the purchase of housing. The lower the ratio, the greater the income that is required; the higher the ratio, the lower the income that is required.

The housing expense and debt ratios change with the market and also with the loan-to-value (LTV) ratio and loan type. For example, as LTV increases, qualifying ratios decrease; adjustable rate mortgages have lower qualifying ratios than do fixed rate mortgages. Because there is so much variation in the qualifying ratios, you should periodically ask an experienced loan officer for the current ratios. Table 8.1 lists the most common ratios as they existed at time of publication: do not use these formulas to estimate a buyer's qualifications until you have verified them with a local lender. A current list of these ratios showing how they are calculated is a useful addition to your buyer's handbook.

Table 8.1 / Common Loan Ratios

CONVENTIONAL LOANS
Maximum Ratios for:

	Conforming Fixed*	Nonoccupant Coborrower	ARMs	
95% LTV	28%	N/A	N/A	income/PITI
	36%			income/debt
80–90% LTV	28%	35%	28%	income/PITI
Under 80%	36%	43%	36%	income/debt
LTV	32%	35%	28%	income/PITI
	38%	43%	36%	income/debt

* Special ratios for conforming/fixed rate loans that apply to the occupants' income and obligations ONLY on loans where there is a nonoccupant coborrower.

FHA LOANS

Any LTV allowed FHA	28%	income/PITI
	41%	income/debt

VA LOANS

Any LTV allowed VA	41% or residual	income/debt

NOTE: Required Ratios, as well as methods for computing qualification, are subject to constant change. The professional buyer's agent should obtain the most up-to-date information from established, competent lenders.

Financial qualifying is the final element of your buyer counseling session. We leave it for last to allow you time to build rapport with your buyers. Only buyers who trust and respect you are likely to answer personal financial questions.

Using a form such as that in Figure 8.1 collect information from the buyers about their gross income and long-term debt. Using this data and the appropriate qualifying ratios, calculate the maximum PITI for which they could qualify. Estimate the taxes and insurance (TI) portion and subtract that amount from the full PITI; the remainder is an estimate of the maxi-

Figure 8.1 / Buyer Income and Debt Information

Borrower	III. BORROWER INFORMATION	Co-Borrower

Borrower's Name (include Jr. or Sr. if applicable) | **Co-Borrower's Name** (include Jr. or Sr. if applicable)

Social Security Number | Home Phone (incl. area code) | DOB (MM/DD/YYYY) | Yrs. School || Social Security Number | Home Phone (incl. area code) | DOB (MM/DD/YYYY) | Yrs. Scho

☐ Married ☐ Unmarried (include single, ☐ Separated divorced, widowed) | Dependents (not listed by Co-Borrower) no. / ages || ☐ Married ☐ Unmarried (include single, ☐ Separated divorced, widowed) | Dependents (not listed by Borrower) no. / ages

Present Address (street, city, state, ZIP) ☐ Own ☐ Rent _____ No. Yrs. | Present Address (street, city, state, ZIP) ☐ Own ☐ Rent _____ No. Yrs

Mailing Address, if different from Present Address | Mailing Address, if different from Present Address

If residing at present address for less than two years, complete the following:

Former Address (street, city, state, ZIP) ☐ Own ☐ Rent _____ No. Yrs. | Former Address (street, city, state, ZIP) ☐ Own ☐ Rent _____ No. Yrs

Borrower	IV. EMPLOYMENT INFORMATION	Co-Borrower

Name & Address of Employer ☐ Self Employed | Yrs. on this job / Yrs. employed in this line of work/profession || Name & Address of Employer ☐ Self Employed | Yrs. on this job / Yrs. employed in this line of work/profession

Position/Title/Type of Business | Business Phone (incl. area code) | Position/Title/Type of Business | Business Phone (incl. area code)

If employed in current position for less than two years or if currently employed in more than one position, complete the following:

Name & Address of Employer ☐ Self Employed | Dates (from – to) / Monthly Income $ || Name & Address of Employer ☐ Self Employed | Dates (from – to) / Monthly Income $

Position/Title/Type of Business | Business Phone (incl. area code) | Position/Title/Type of Business | Business Phone (incl. area code)

Name & Address of Employer ☐ Self Employed | Dates (from – to) / Monthly Income $ || Name & Address of Employer ☐ Self Employed | Dates (from – to) / Monthly Income $

Position/Title/Type of Business | Business Phone (incl. area code) | Position/Title/Type of Business | Business Phone (incl. area code)

V. MONTHLY INCOME AND COMBINED HOUSING EXPENSE INFORMATION

Gross Monthly Income	Borrower	Co-Borrower	Total	Combined Monthly Housing Expense	Present	Proposed
Base Empl. Income*	$	$	$ 0	Rent	$	
Overtime			0	First Mortgage (P&I)		$
Bonuses			0	Other Financing (P&I)		
Commissions			0	Hazard Insurance		
Dividends/Interest			0	Real Estate Taxes		
Net Rental Income			0	Mortgage Insurance		
Other (before completing, see the notice in "describe other income," below)			0	Homeowner Assn. Dues		
			0	Other:		
Total	$ 0	$ 0	$ 0	Total	$ 0	$ 0.00

* Self Employed Borrower(s) may be required to provide additional documentation such as tax returns and financial statements.

Describe Other Income *Notice:* Alimony, child support, or separate maintenance income need not be revealed if the Borrower (B) or Co-Borrower (C) does not choose to have it considered for repaying this loan.

B/C		Monthly Amount
		$

Excerpted from the Standard FNMA/FHLMC Loan Application Form.

mum monthly principal and interest (PI) for which the buyers can qualify. With a financial calculator or mortgage tables and current interest rates, convert this PI payment to the equivalent mortgage amount.

At this point, ask the buyers how they feel about the PITI payment maximum you have just calculated. Listen carefully to their responses, remembering that their interests come first and that you are acting as a counselor. This is important because many buyers, at least initially, do not want to pay the maximum for which they can qualify although, after seeing properties in a lower price range, many also find themselves increasing that range to the maximum. Whatever PI amount the buyers decide on, calculate the equivalent mortgage amount.

Regardless of whether the buyers express comfort with the maximum PITI or wish to reduce the payment to a lower amount, you now need to explore their cash reserves to determine the maximum amount they are willing to invest in a property. Buyers may not be willing to invest all their cash in real estate. This is *their* decision; accept whatever they tell you and add it onto the mortgage amount to obtain an approximate maximum sales price.

Some buyers do not have the luxury of deciding how much cash they want to invest and, instead, need every available penny and may even need to tap noncash resources and possibly gifts from family. To assist you in working with buyers who have limited resources, see Figure 8.2, which lists ways to (1) increase cash, (2) increase income, and (3) reduce debt.

Today, the most important question in mortgage financing is "What is their/his/her credit score?" Most lenders have carved-in-stone rules about FICO (Fairm Isaac and Co. of San Rafael, California, who invented the mathematical formula for credit scoring) credit scores (which range from 350 to 900): their best rates are

Figure 8.2 / Ways to Increase Cash, Increase Income, and Decrease Debt

When working with buyers who have limited resources, buyers' agents will find the following lists useful in helping their buyers qualify.

Sources of Cash

1. Existing savings accounts
2. Borrowing from relatives
3. Waiting until money is saved
4. Proceeds from sale of current home
5. Gift from relative
6. Part-time job
7. Borrowing against whole-life insurance policy
8. Selling assets
9. Selling odds and ends at garage sale/flea market
10. Arranging with employer to receive bonuses or relocation allowance in advance
11. Obtaining advances on other sources of income, e.g., leases, patents, copyrights, income tax refund
12. Removing equity from property not yet sold via bridge loan, financing car, stocks
13. Personal loan from major credit card, credit union, finance company, letter of credit, friends
14. Security deposit refund
15. Rent paid in advance, mortgage debt in arrears = "free" month
16. Closing at end of month to reduce closing costs
17. Financing closing costs
18. "Sweat equity" personal labor prior to closing

Figure 8.2 / Ways to Increase Cash, Increase Income,
and Decrease Debt (continued)

Sources of Income

1. Scheduled/regular cost-of-living and merit pay increases which employer will verify, in writing
2. In-kind income or fringe benefits, e.g., company car, expense account
3. Part-time job with sustained employment of six months or more
4. Income from other sources, e.g., VA education benefits, cosigner or coborrower
5. When buying multifamily property, getting tenants to sign lease in advance (about 75 percent of rent counts toward income)
6. Taking reduced standard income tax deduction

Reducing Debt

1. Paying it off
2. Selling items with outstanding loans
3. Transferring debt to a relative, friend, or employer
4. Refinancing existing debt to obtain a lower monthly payment
5. Leasing car instead of buying and arranging for the car lease/dealer company to take the old car as a trade and pay off debt
6. Recognizing that debt does not count when there are fewer than six months remaining

offered to borrowers with a score of 700 or higher. If your buyers' score is 698, those two points could cost them thousands of dollars as the interest rate difference between these two scores is about one-half percentage point. If their scores fall below 675, the rate can go up another 1.2 percent. The best advice you can give your clients is to pay their bills on time, keep account balances low, and take out new credit only when they need it! Should your clients' scores be too low, recommend that, in addition to your advice, they plan now to pay off account balances and correct any errors they find on the credit report their lender orders. Add them to your database and keep in touch as they go through this process as they can become very loyal buyers. Also read the section in Chapter 6 titled "Credit-Impaired Buyers."

Hazard Insurance

As recently as the early 2000s, obtaining hazard insurance was easy. By 2003–2004, it became so difficult that many purchase contracts contained a contingency allowing buyers to satisfy themselves that they could both review the Comprehensive Loss Underwriting Exchange (CLUE) report on the property and actually obtain hazard insurance. CLUE reports are available upon the request of either the seller or an insurance agent. These reports detail the property's claims history for the most recent five years. Insurers may use this information to deny coverage so (a) make the sale contingent on a home inspection that ensures that the problems identified in the CLUE report have been repaired and (b) make the contract conditional upon the buyer being able to obtain a policy (not a "binder") at closing in an amount under $\_x\_$ (this number depends on the local market).

It should also be pointed out that the buyer himself/herself may present a problem in obtaining insurance. The insurance companies have determined that the lower the buyer's FICO score, the more likely the person is to use insurance for maintenance, rather than just for catastrophes.

It is critically important that you advise your buyers to obtain sufficient coverage, as many homes today are underinsured. Marshall & Swift/Boeckh, a Los Angeles company that insurers rely on for help in calculating the value of houses, estimates that 64 percent of American homes are underinsured by an average of 27 percent, with some homes underinsured by 60 percent or more. Part of this is because old policies that were called "guaranteed replacement policies" have been replaced with "extended replacement policies" that pay the amount stated on the policy plus, typically, an additional 20 percent to 25 percent. Another part is because the nationwide housing boom of the late 1990s and early 2000s has been rapidly driving up the cost of lumber, bricks, cement, and other construction material (by more than the "built-in escalator" that simply keeps pace with general inflation). And, finally, many insurance agents often lack the training to assess accurately the value of a home and usually rely on a computer program rather than actually leaving their offices to assess a house personally.

There is another insurance problem about which buyers' agents need to advise their clients: increasingly insurance carriers are adding exclusions to their policies, including damage from pests, floods, earthquakes, mold, war, and outside water and ice. At the same time, premiums for coverage in areas/states that suffer frequent wildfires (e.g., California) and hurricanes (e.g., Florida) have increased substantially. These inclusions and locational premium increases make the buyer's inspection clause critically important. Advise your buyer clients to use the time between contract signature and the inspection objection deadline to educate themselves about both what is and is not covered by their insurance policies and what the common risks are for the area and home they are purchasing. They should hire specialized inspectors for any of these uninsurable risks such as pest threats, radon, and mold.

Because of these numerous problems, the buyer needs to start searching for homeowner's insurance as soon as the buyer starts the buying process. Counsel the buyer that the premium for a hazard policy may be far too expensive and will throw the buyer's ratios out of line.

Inspection Information

The items consist of

- a sample survey, appraisal, and home inspection report (identifying information removed);
- information about typical tests (e.g., termites, radon); and
- a list of inspection companies you highly recommend.

Discuss the kind of information obtained from each of these items. With the inspection report, emphasize that the buyers will be looking for red flags and not for detail, which simply indicates normal wear and tear that, if desired, they can repair after buying the property.

Survey/ Improvement Location Certificate (ILC)

Explain to your buyer clients that surveys/ILCs illustrate the property boundaries and the location of the improvements (house, fences, sheds, etc.) within those boundaries. In the past, a survey/ILC was generally a requirement of the company that insures the title to the property: they and your buyers want to know if there are any easements and/or encroachments.

Today fences, sheds, garages, and so on, sometimes encroach on a neighboring property, especially in subdivisions and yet many lenders no longer require surveys/ILCs because of both the cost to the buyer and the fact that such problems are relatively uncommon. As a result, the title companies in turn often don't require surveys/ILCs *even* when it is a condition of the purchase contract. As a buyer's agent, you must discuss this situation with your client; we strongly recommend that you advise your client to demand a survey/ILC prior to closing. Assuming the client follows your advice, inform both the lender and the title company.

Real Estate Attorneys

Include a list of several (ideally more than two) attorneys who specialize in real estate law; include their telephone numbers. Preparation of this list must be based on either your personal experience or the attorneys' reputation for being deal makers rather than deal breakers. Discuss the seriousness and legality of the transaction into which the buyers are about to enter and recommend that all legal documents be reviewed by an attorney before being finalized. Differentiate between legal advice and the advice and information buyers need about such factors as price, location, construction, and negotiating strategy. Advice on these latter items should not be defined as "legal"; therefore, such advice does not require the services of an attorney.

PROBABLE EVENTS AND TIMING

At this point in the counseling session, most buyers will be overwhelmed by the details that you have just presented. It is thus advisable to simplify matters by reviewing a single-sheet outline of the probable transaction events and their timing. Emphasize who is responsible for each event: you as agent, some other professional involved in the transaction (lender, appraiser, title company, etc.), and the seller or the buyer.

This is an opportune time to bring up the critical nature of each date that will appear in the final purchase contract. Tell the buyers that "time is of the essence" and that a formal extension agreement will be used should it be impossible to meet any date. However, meeting contract dates is always preferable, because any change, no matter how small, does give the other party the right to refuse to change and possibly cancel the contract.

This portion of the counseling appointment is not designed to frighten the buyers. It is intended to give buyers a realistic vision of the events that are about to occur and impress upon them the serious nature of such events while simultaneously letting the buyers know that they will need professional help (your help!) to complete the transaction successfully.

FIGURE 8.3 / Probable Events and Timing for a Typical Residential Purchase

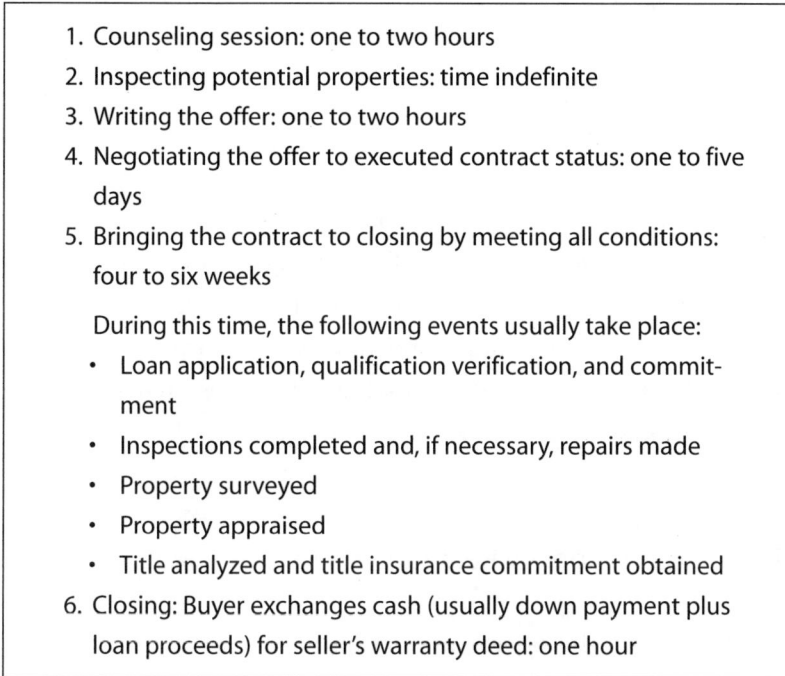

1. Counseling session: one to two hours
2. Inspecting potential properties: time indefinite
3. Writing the offer: one to two hours
4. Negotiating the offer to executed contract status: one to five days
5. Bringing the contract to closing by meeting all conditions: four to six weeks

   During this time, the following events usually take place:
   - Loan application, qualification verification, and commitment
   - Inspections completed and, if necessary, repairs made
   - Property surveyed
   - Property appraised
   - Title analyzed and title insurance commitment obtained
6. Closing: Buyer exchanges cash (usually down payment plus loan proceeds) for seller's warranty deed: one hour

Figure 8.3 is a sample probable events and timing outline. Modify it as necessary to fit your normal transactions. Add this as the next page in your buyer's handbook.

DISCLOSURE AND THE AGENCY REPRESENTATION DECISION

Based on the factors (company agency policy, your relationship to the buyers, your expertise, and your time requirements) discussed in Chapter 5, by now you will have decided whether you want to offer client status in this particular instance. Assuming that you do, this is the ideal point in the counseling session to discuss agency. Your dialogue should include the elements that follow.

The Disclosure

Disclose that traditionally many real estate agents working with buyers represented the seller during the buyer's purchase of a home, but that in today's market, most agents work for buyers, representing them, and that is what you want to offer them. In states that allow dual agency, designated agency, and/or nonagency, disclose these options as well.

Defining the Agency Relationship

Make sure the buyers understand that the agency relationship results from *mutual consent* between both principal (buyer) and agent that the agent will *act on the principal's behalf* and *subject to his or her control.* Tell the buyers that by the regulations and/or law of your state, you and all other real estate licensees must act as agents of either the buyer or the seller or, if dual agency is allowed, both in every transaction (except in those states that allow nonagency).

Further describe the agency relationship as one in which the agent owes fiduciary or statutory duties to his or her principal. Define these duties as loyalty, obedience, disclosure, confidentiality, reasonable care and diligence, and accounting for all monies and property entrusted to the agent. As you discuss these duties, use examples, preferably from your own experience, of how the duty might be applied in a real estate transaction. For example, *confidentiality* means that you, as the buyer's agent, will not tell the seller or the seller's agent the highest price the buyer will pay; similarly, *loyalty* means that you will tell the buyer anything you know about the seller and/or the seller's property that might make the buyer's negotiating position stronger or weaker (provided you did not learn such information in a prior agency relationship with the seller).

The agency relationship and resultant fiduciary duties should be the next page in your buyer presentation book.

Describing the Buyer's Right to Be Represented

For most people, a home is the most expensive and significant purchase they have ever made. They have a right to be represented in that transaction. Continue by telling the buyer that the seller is represented by his or her listing agent and that it is your preference and your company's policy, when you work with buyers, to represent those buyers.

If your company policy allows dual agency for in-house sales or, in some states, designated agency, disclose now what would happen in a disclosed dual agency/designated agency relationship. For most companies, *dual agency/designated agency* means that the agents will neither disclose to the buyer the lowest price the seller will take nor disclose to the seller the highest price the buyer will pay. In addition, because in any given situation there may be additional terms that the buyer and/or seller require to be confidential, such terms will be specified in the dual agency/designated agency addendum to both the buyer agency contract and the seller's listing contract. Tell the buyer that no facts *about* the property may be kept confidential by the seller and that all such facts must be disclosed to the buyer.

If your state law and company policy allow designated/appointed agency should the buyer want to purchase a company listing, explain how this relationship works. If the buyer is interested in your personal listing, we strongly recommend that you either treat the buyer as a customer (with full disclosure of the ramifications) or refer them to an agent either in your company or a different company.

Soliciting Questions

Ask the buyers if they have any questions, and if they understand all that you have just discussed. At this point, keep quiet, wait, and listen. Deal with any questions and concerns expressed until you sense comprehension. Unless the buyers' reactions are negative, in which case you need to decide whether you want to pursue working with them, proceed to the next step.

Reviewing the Contract

Place the buyer agency contract in front of the buyers. Review each part with them in sufficient detail to obtain informed consent as to its content and intent, asking for oral agreement at the end of each section. At the end of the contract review, either (1) hand the buyers a pen and show them where to sign (if you have done an adequate job in the preceding portions of your counseling appointment, this assumptive close will result in the signatures you want and initiate your buyer agency relationship) or (2) invite them to review the contract further with their attorney or on their own, but remind them that it must be signed before you show any property. (See the forms appendix at the end of the book for a sample buyer agency contract.)

TRAINING THE BUYER CLIENT

Because client status is often a new position for buyers, they will need some training in how to behave toward you and other agents they may encounter. The best time to begin the education process is right after the buyer agency contract is presented.

Remind the buyers that you, your broker, and all the other agents in your company represent them (except in designated agency in which you—and possibly your broker—are the *only* agents who represent the buyer) and will hold their interests as primary (equal in the case of dual agency). Tell them that for you to do the best possible job for them, they should confide in you, sharing their honest reactions to the properties inspected and the reasons for their likes and dislikes. You will, as their agent, give them your professional advice on all aspects of the transaction and be their advocate in dealings with the seller and the seller's agent. Should you, for some reason, not be available, they should feel comfortable in working instead with your broker or some other agent who is handling your business in your absence.

Because many buyers, regardless of their agency status, will continue to visit open houses and call on signs and ads, you also need to discuss how your buyers should relate to other agents. Tell them that there is nothing wrong with such activities but that should they contact other agents, they should first identify themselves as your client. Give them several of your business cards and ask them to hand one to the host at any open house they visit.

Even with your coaching, contact between your buyer client and other agents has a strong potential for misunderstanding. Therefore, it is best to encourage your clients to notify you of any signs and ads they find interesting so that you can find the information they want, thus saving them both the trouble of making multiple calls and the potential liability of miscommunication. If they do visit open houses without you, train them to first ask permission of the host to inspect the house without you after having introduced themselves as your client. Should the host object, warn them to politely leave because there is a potential liability for a double commission should they proceed and then decide to purchase the property. If the host does not object, warn them not to show any exceptional interest and ask them to contact you immediately if they do find a property they especially like. Ideally, of course, you always will be with them when they inspect open houses as well as all other properties.

DETERMINING WANTS AND NEEDS

The old saying that "buyers are liars" can apply as easily to buyer clients as to buyer customers if you do not both adequately determine their wants and needs and remain constantly sensitive to their reactions. Rather than being liars, buyers are simply people who often have not thoroughly examined their own likes and dislikes. Such an analysis is something you need to help them do.

In general, the best clues to the buyers' wants and needs are their memories of both their last home and the home in which they grew up. Ask each buyer to visualize those homes and list the aspects that he or she really liked and really disliked. If there is more than one buyer, ask each to do this exercise separately.

Next, ask the buyer to visualize an ideal home and describe it in terms of location, general appearance, and specific characteristics of some or even all of the rooms. Again, if there is more than one buyer, ask each to do this exercise separately. Use a form like Figure 8.4. Ideally, there will be sufficient time for the buyers to do these exercises in a relaxed manner, without interruptions. So that you can understand their wants and needs, ask that the lists be put in writing and returned to you before the first appointment to inspect potential properties. When you receive the lists, review them for differences and similarities between the buyers, if there is more than one, and also between the present home and the home in which each buyer grew up and/or last lived.

Discuss these differences and similarities with the buyers. Then, together, prepare a list of likes and dislikes. Ask the buyers to rank the items on each list so that you can use the lists when setting up showing appointments. Pay particular attention to only the first two or three items on each list; lower-ranked characteristics are rarely significant in the buying decision. Thus, the exercise of setting priorities effectively separates needs from wants and, for buyers in the higher price

Figure 8.4 / Prioritize Your Wants and Needs

HOUSE HUNTING CHECKLIST
Prioritize Your Wants and Needs

The home features you want aren't always the same as the ones you need. Use this checklist to help separate needs from wants. And consider how you'll live in the house today and in years to come as you accommodate growing children and elderly parents.

N   W   DW   TYPE
- Single-family
- Townhome
- Condo
- New
- Existing

N   W   DW   LOCATION
- Central city
- Suburbs
- Outlying
- Flooring
- Away from heavy traffic

NEAR
- Job
- Schools
- Parks
- Public transportation
- Airport
- Expressway
- Neighborhood shopping
- Regional mall
- Entertainment/restaurants/theaters

N   W   DW   CONDITION
- Well kept
- Fixer-upper
- Needs minor work

N   W   DW   KITCHEN
- Countertop material:_____
- Newer appliances
- Eating area
- Desk area
- Pantry
- Center Island

N   W   DW   SYSTEMS
- Boiler, furnace oil tank (circle perferred system)
- Central AC
- Security
- Internet/cable ready

N   W   DW   FLOOR PLAN
- Basement
- Finished basement
- Attic
- Formal foyer
- Formal living room
- Great room
- Family room
- Formal dining room
- Office
- Media room/rec room
- Mud room/laundry room

N   W   DW   BATHROOMS
- Number:_____
- Shower
- Tub
- Double sinks
- Dressing area

N   W   DW   STYLE
- Traditional
- Contemporary
- Ranch
- Two-story
- Tudor
- Victorian
- Split-level
- Colonial
- Other_____

Figure 8.4 / Prioritize Your Wants and Needs (continued)

N	W	DW	BEDROOMS
■			Number:_____
			Master suite
			First floor master suite
			Rooms for future children/elderly relatives

N	W	DW	EXTERIOR
			Brick
			Stucco
			Aluminum siding
			Vinyl siding
			Wood frames

N	W	DW	GARAGE/PARKING
■			Size:_____
			Street parking
			Paved driveway
			Reserved or deeded spot (for condos)

SPECIAL FEATURES

N	W	DW	INTERIOR
			Fireplace
			Vaulted ceilings
			High ceilings
			Wood floors
			Built-in cabinets
			Big closets
			Extra storage space
			Whirlpool/hot tub
			First/second-floor laundry

N	W	DW	COMMUNITY/ NEIGHBORHOOD
■			
			Highly-rated schools
			Swimming pool
			Tennis courts
			Golf course
			Parks
			Park programs/activities
			Health club
			Sidewalks
			Local college

N	W	DW	EXTERIOR
			Good view
			Natural light
			Backyard
			Garden
			Play area
			Screened porch
			Patio/deck
			Barbecue area
			Outdoor lighting
			Fenced yard
			Mature trees
			Mature shrubs
			Maintenance provided by a homeowners association

N	W	DW	LIFESTYLE
			Kid-friendly spaces
			Room for older parents
			Sport/basketball court
			Room for guests/ entertaining

ranges, critical likes and dislikes from those that would be "nice but not necessary."

After you have seen several properties that match the buyers' likes and dislikes, if no property catches their attention, review both lists again and ask the buyers to rerank the items based on their recent experience in looking at properties.

It should not be necessary to inspect more than about ten (fewer for Internet buyers) properties if this step is done well. Remember that your time and that of the buyers is precious: spending sufficient time on analysis in the initial counseling session will save countless hours of driving around looking at properties that the buyers quickly discard. If you have helped your buyers to accurately analyze their likes and dislikes, and you select properties to show based on that analysis, your reputation as a true professional will grow significantly.

THE BUYER AGENCY AGREEMENT

The buyer agency agreement closely parallels the seller's listing contract: it is a binding agreement between agent and client that describes the terms under which the buyer will both purchase real estate and compensate the agent for certain services performed. Like the seller's listing contract, there are several types of buyer agency agreements that have similar components and, to a greater or lesser extent, ensure client loyalty.

Types of Buyer Agency Agreements

Buyer agency agreements can take several forms: exclusive right, exclusive agency, or open contracts. Most fall into the exclusive right category. Although this certainly is the preferable version from a commission assurance standpoint, there are good reasons to use either of the others as well.

Exclusive Right Agreements. This agreement, when signed, binds the buyers to compensate their agent whenever they purchase a property of the type described within the time period given. Unless otherwise restricted, the property can be MLS-listed, for-sale-by-owner, or otherwise unlisted; it can be new or used, constructed, or only planned. In return for such complete loyalty, the buyers should expect from their agent professional advice and advocacy, full exercise of the agent's fiduciary/statutory duties, and prompt and wholehearted attention.

Exclusive Agency Agreements. This agreement assures the agent of buyer loyalty relative to any other agents. However, it gives the buyers the flexibility to purchase property on their own without the assistance of an agent and thus without any compensation being due to their agent. Such an arrangement may be preferred by experienced buyers who generally do not need or want advice and advocacy but want the insurance of knowing they have a reliable consultant, should they need one, as well as access to listed properties. Agents who sign these agreements are well advised to work on a retainer/hourly fee basis that may or may not be credited against any success fee earned.

Open Agreements. Under the terms of an open agreement, the buyers can work with more than one buyer's agent at the same time but owe you compensation only if they use your services. Such an agreement is preferred by those buyers who definitely want representation but may not be sure of property location or type and know that agent expertise may vary with these factors. These buyers, therefore, want the flexibility to use more than one agent. Perhaps the best example is the knowledgeable commercial investor or user who has his or her "own" agent in each of several commercial real estate companies, who understands the special expertise and knowledge of each of those agents, and who recognizes that because commercial properties often are not listed on an MLS, each company will have its own semiprivate inventory of properties. Another example of open agency occurs whenever an agency relationship is established by signature on a disclosure form only, as commonly occurs in California as well as other states. Again, the agent here is well advised to use a retainer and/or hourly fee, which is usually credited against any success fee. It should be remembered that with just a signed disclosure form (open agency), buyers are not legally committed to paying fees.

Written Versus Oral Agreements

In some states, court decisions (and thus common law) and/or statutory law and/or regulations clearly require that any buyer agency relationship must be committed to writing; Colorado is a good example of this statutory requirement. Without a written contract between buyer and agent, the law presumes that the agent is working for the seller as either the listing agent or working for neither as a nonagent, or in some states such as Illinois and Louisiana, that you are the agent of the person with whom you are working. However, even in the absence of statute, regulation, and/or relevant court decisions, it is strongly recommended that any buyer agency agreement be in writing. An oral agreement is usually not defensible and cannot be relied upon to ensure payment of your commission.

Major Components of a Buyer Agency Contract

Regardless of which type of buyer agency contract is used, several major components should appear in any agreement.

Identification of the Parties. Both the broker and the buyer must be adequately named and described. As is true of a seller's listing contract, the agreement is the property of the broker and is in the company name rather than in the name of the agent who is working directly for the buyer client. Similarly, if the buyer is other than an individual, any additional buyers should be named, and if the buyer is a corporation or a partnership, it should be named and the individual with binding signature authority should be identified.

Property Type Description. This description should be reasonably general in its character, for it is the intent that has significance, not the specifics. The type, residential or commercial, should be identified along with a short description of the desired property's character. In addition, the general location, an approximate price range, and preferred terms should be indicated. If there are any specifics for the buyer that are absolutes, these should be detailed. The adequacy of this section depends in large part on your success in determining the buyer's wants and needs during the buyer counseling session. However, especially if you make the description detailed, be prepared to modify it with an amend/extend agreement whenever your buyer clients change their specific requirements.

Compensation and Method of Payment. Ideally, the contract will allow for retainer, hourly, and/or success fees. The first two should have the option of being credited against any success fee. The success fee can be either a flat fee or a percentage based on either the list or the sales price.

Contracts usually require that payment of any success fee be made at closing. They may further stipulate that the buyer's agent must first seek payment from the transaction before looking to the buyer client for direct compensation. (For a detailed discussion of buyers' agents' fees and compensation, see Chapter 10 that points out that percentage fees are a conflict of interest for buyers' agents and must therefore be discussed with the buyer client.)

Term of Agreement. To be legally effective, any contract must include dates for both commencement and termination. The duration, which is negotiable between agent and buyer client, will depend on the type of property desired, current market conditions, and any of the buyer's specific requirements.

It is strongly recommended that a termination clause be included in the Additional Provisions section. We have found that buyers feel much more comfortable knowing they can easily opt out and are therefore more willing to sign the contract.

Disclosure of Any Potential Conflict of Interest. The buyer agency agreement should require that the agent will immediately disclose to the buyer any possible conflicting interests. Such conflicts would include, but not be limited to, agent ownership, in part or full, of the property in question, an agency relationship with the property's seller, company ownership of the title and/or mortgage providers, and working with another buyer who is interested in the same property. Disclosure by itself is not enough; the agreement should further stipulate the events that will occur in the event of any such conflict. These events would include termination of the agreement or institution of a disclosed dual agency/designated agency. (See also Chapter 5.)

The contract components described above represent the bare minimum. In addition, the buyer agency agreement should also describe the contract's effect (i.e., a description of whether it is an exclusive right, exclusive agency, or an open agency contract) and may include terms for termination by the parties, disclosure of the buyer's identity, indemnification of the broker, assignment of the contract, and many other contingencies. See the forms appendix at the end of the book for a model buyer agency agreement: this is a sample only and should not be used for any purpose without review and acceptance by your legal counsel.

SUMMARY

The buyer counseling session is of great importance and, unfortunately, is the step most frequently skipped. Since every buyer is different, no two counseling sessions will ever be the same. Rarely does the session include the ideal level of detail specified in this chapter. The ideal, however, should be your goal: the closer you come to this goal, the more effective, efficient, and professional you will be as a buyer's agent. As with most human endeavors, adequate preparation is the major cause of success.

The buyer counseling session will require a minimum of one hour of uninterrupted time. It should occur before any properties are shown or any serious discussions take place. Use of a buyer's handbook or a PowerPoint equivalent is essential.

Effective buyer counseling consists of six major parts: (1) building rapport and trust, (2) introducing probable transaction events and timing, (3) agency disclosure and the representation decision, (4) training the buyer client, (5) determining the buyer's wants and needs, and (6) financial qualifying.

In most instances, a successful buyer counseling session will lead to the signing of a buyer agency contract. This document is very similar in character to a seller's listing contract. It may be an exclusive right contract between agent and client, an exclusive agency agreement, or an open agency agreement. In any case, it should include at least the following components: identification of buyer and broker, description of the property type, compensation and method of payment, term of agreement, and required disclosure of any conflict of interest.

Some states mandate that buyer agency contracts be in writing. Without such an agreement, it is presumed that the agent working with the buyer is the seller's agent or a nonagent.

Because most buyer agency contracts are exclusive right in character, the effect of such an agreement is clear: provided that the terms of purchase reflect the requirements of the agreement, the buyer's agent will be compensated. The agreement, therefore, ensures buyer loyalty!

REVIEW QUESTIONS

1. Your agency relationship should be disclosed to
   a.   the buyer.
   b.   the seller.
   c.   any other agents involved in the transaction.
   d.   All of the above

ANSWER:

d. Agency relationships should/must be disclosed to everyone involved in a transaction.

2. The buyer counseling session should
   a.   be brief.
   b.   take place concurrent with signing the purchase contract.
   c.   emphasize adversarial relationships.
   d.   None of the above

ANSWER:

d. The buyer counseling session usually requires one to two hours and is not brief. It occurs before any significant action such as showing homes, or writing offers is taken. It results in a partnership between agent and client. When discussing how negotiations will occur, a win-win relationship rather than adversarial is stressed.

3. Which is not true of the buyer's handbook?
   a. Includes copies of both buyer agency agreements and purchase contracts
   b. Consists of a number of documents
   c. Assists in building rapport and trust between agent and buyer
   d. Is given as a gift at closing

ANSWER:

d. The buyer's handbook is given to the buyer during the buyer counseling session. It includes copies of contracts as well as other documents and is designed to assist in building rapport and trust between agent and buyer through sharing the agent's knowledge and expertise.

4. A feeling of rapport and trust between buyer and agent
   a. separates top producers from all other agents.
   b. is fragile and easily destroyed.
   c. once established cannot be destroyed.
   d. is not related to the agent's experience, education, and training.

ANSWER:

b. Rapport and trust is a feeling and therefore fragile; it can easily be destroyed through miscommunication and inattention. Although the ability to create this feeling is characteristic of top producers, any agent can develop the ability. However, this ability is usually developed through experience as well as education and training.

5. Which should not be included in the buyer's handbook?
   a. Seller's financial statement
   b. List of real estate attorneys
   c. Community and school information
   d. Sample documents

ANSWER:

a. The buyer's handbook includes many sections including (b), (c), and (d). However, it would not include information about the seller's financial statement because the buyer's agent would not have access to this information (if he or she did, it should probably be included!).

6. As a buyer's agent, your agency discussion with the buyer should include which of the following?
   a. Buyer's right to be represented
   b. In-house sales and your company's policy toward it
   c. Your company's agency policy
   d. All of the above

ANSWER:

d. Although items (a), (b), and (c) may seem like too much legalese, these items are all critically important to the buyer's understanding of the transaction and what he or she can expect from the agent. The fact that it is the buyer's right to be represented is a good introduction to the discussion of in-house sales and company policy.

7. The exclusive buyer agency agreement should include
   a. events in the case of a conflict of interest.
   b. compensation and method of payment.
   c. term of the agreement.
   d. All of the above

ANSWER:

d. All of these items as well as many more are necessary parts of the buyer agency agreement.

8. Which of the following is NOT a reason for a buyer's agent to calculate the buyer's financial qualifications?
   a. Determine whether the buyer qualifies for an owner-carried loan
   b. Negotiate with the seller and/or the seller's agent
   c. Estimate the price range of properties to be shown
   d. Show the buyer what information should not be disclosed to the lender

ANSWER:

d. Although many agents today do not estimate the buyer's ability to qualify for a loan because there are so many variations, it's important to do a rough calculation during the counseling session for the reasons given in (a), (b), and (c); (d) is not a good reason because a buyer's agent should encourage his or her client to disclose all relevant information to the lender.

9. Mary, a buyer's agent, represents two different buyers, Mr. and Mrs. Jones and Albert Einstein. Both buyers, after seeing a number of properties each, decide that they want to make an offer on the same house.
   a. What should Mary do?
   b. Should Mary have shown both buyers the same property?

ANSWERS:

a. Mary should disclose this fact to both buyers and obtain agreement from each that she'll not disclose the terms of one buyer's offer to the other buyer.

b. Yes, Mary should have shown both buyers the same property; it is her obligation to show buyer clients all properties that meet their requirements. However, the possibility of both buyers wanting to purchase the same property should have been covered in the buyer agency agreement.

CHAPTER 9

Showing and Closing Properties

Locating and showing properties is often more intensive and time consuming for the buyer's agent than it is for the seller's agent or the nonagent. This is because the buyer's agent is in no way limited to listed properties and may even be contacting property owners who have shown no formal interest in selling.

Likewise, the showing process is not just a critical part of selling. Rather, it becomes a cooperative venture between the buyer client and the agent in which the agent points out not only each property's strengths but also its weaknesses. This practice allows the buyer to make a truly informed choice.

LOCATING THE PROPERTY

After the thorough counseling session discussed in Chapter 8, the buyer's agent should be well prepared to begin locat-

Figure 9.1 / Sample Contact Letter

REAL ESTATE SERVICES, LTD.
9876 Main St.
Boulder, CO 80302
303/555-3335
303/555-3325   Fax

March 31, 2005

Mr. and Mrs. _____
743 Same Street
Boulder, Colorado 80302

I am the agent of Mr. and Mrs. _____, a young professional couple who have just moved to Boulder from Texas. They want to buy a home and are primarily interested in the Mapleton Hill area. For the past several months, I have shown them every property on the market, but they have not been able to find one that meets their needs.

As a result, we began looking at properties that are not currently on the market, but that, from the outside, seemed to be what they want. Your home at 743 Aspen Street appears to be just that and they, therefore, have instructed me to prepare a market analysis for them as well as the enclosed contract, which is based on that analysis. They are very serious, as you can see from both the contract and the copy of their $10,000 earnest money check.

We realize that your home is not listed; however, we are hopeful that you might be interested in selling now or at some time in the near future. We would like to talk with you to obtain your reaction and discuss the contract and sugest 10:00 A.M. on Thursday, April 7, 2005. If this is not convenient with you, please call me at 303-555-3335 to set another time; if we do not hear from you, we'll be at your door at 10:00 A.M. on Thursday. To assist you in preparing for our meeting, I've also enclosed a copy of the market analysis, which is based on properties that have recently sold in the Mapleton Hill area.

Thank you in advance for the consideration you will give to our contract. We very much look forward to meeting and talking with you.

Sincerely,
REAL ESTATE SERVICES, LTD.

Jane Doe, Broker

JD:AJK
Enclosures

ing potential properties for the buyer client. Using the specific criteria from the buyer, the buyer's agent begins the search for potential properties from a number of different sources.

Buyers' agents need not be limited to the multiple-listing service (MLS) or their own or company listings; you should also consider properties that are for-sale-by-owner (FSBO) and those for which there is no indication that the owner desires a sale. Figure 9.1 is an example of a letter used to contact such owners. You should also check advertising in newspapers, relevant Internet sites including lists of foreclosure properties, and other publications without being concerned about whether such properties are listed since your buyer agency agreement should describe how you will be compensated in such situations.

Because buyers' agents represent buyers, there is no question as to their agency status. However, a seller's agent or nonagent working with a buyer customer who attempts to buy an FSBO must realize that the owner has not made the blanket unilateral offer of compensation. Thus, there is neither a listing agreement nor a commission arrangement. In effect, unless the seller's agent or nonagent goes through the entire listing process, he or she is working with two unrepresented parties, the buyer and the seller, and can be in a very risky situation. In this situation, it is important to remember that both the FSBO seller and the agent's buyer customer should get legal advice before signing any agreement or contract.

The buyer's agent, on the other hand, has much more flexibility in working with unlisted sellers and can handle the commission in any of the ways described in Chapter 10, provided that there is appropriate disclosure, documentation, and informed consent. Frequently, FSBOs are more than willing to

Figure 9.2 / Sample Buyer Agency Disclosure Form and Commission
Agreement

FAX TRANSMITTAL: Please deliver promptly!

BUYER AGENCY DISCLOSURE TO REALTOR®
and
COMMISSION AGREEMENT

TO:

Listing Company	Listing Agent
Phone Number	Fax Number

FROM:

Agent	Agent
Phone No.	Phone No.

DATE: _____

RE: _____
Property Address

_____, acting through its above-referenced associate
(Agent), is serving as an agent representing

The/Mr./Ms. _____ (the "Buyer").
(Last Name)

Both you and the Seller should understand that as a Buyer's agent in this transaction the Agent has the duty to act on behalf of the Buyer and will not be acting on behalf of the Seller.

This duty requires that all information regarding this transaction which is given to the Agent by you or the Seller be disclosed to the Buyer. For example, if you disclose to the Agent that your Seller is compelled by outside circumstances to sell by a certain date, or that your Seller is prepared to lower the price, the Agent would be required to disclose this information to the Buyer. Please keep this in mind when communicating with the Agent.

We have scheduled a showing with the Buyer for:

_____   _____
Showing Date   Time

It is our understanding that our fee will be paid by the Seller through your agreeing to pay us a commission equal to the commission you are offering to pay a subagent who procures a buyer for the property or the co-operative fee offered to a buyer's agent as shown in the "MLS". So that our files will be complete, we would appreciate your indicating your agreement to our showing the property on the basis indicated above by signing below and returning a copy to Agent (if possible, fax to number reflected above). Even without receiving the acknowledgement, we will assume you agree to the showing and commission arrangement described unless you notify us to the contrary within 24 hours of your receipt of this disclosure.

_____   _____
Listing Broker Signature   Date

Source: Fox & Lazo, Inc. REALTORS®.

pay a selling agent's fee, and this is particularly true with a buyer's agent. In this situation, buyers' agents are well advised to obtain a commission agreement from the FSBO prior to showing (see Figure 9.2).

With regard to listed properties, buyers' agents, according to the NAR Model MLS Rules and Regulations, have complete access to the MLS as long as they are members of the MLS, are current with their payments, and are in good standing. (If an MLS restricts participation of buyers' agents, it is contrary to NAR policy; there are few, if any, such MLSs in today's market.) Most important, the MLS is a "blanket unilateral offer of compensation" that clearly states the selling fee offered to buyers' agents as well as to any other member.

The *NAR Handbook on Multiple Listing Policy,* Section 7.40, "MLS Participation by Brokers Acting as Agents of Potential Purchasers," makes it quite clear that buyers' agents have the right to participate in the MLS in the same way as any other MLS member. (In the past, there was occasional mention of a possible conflict of interest arising out of disclosure of the "confidential" information in the MLS to buyers' agents. However, this has been deemed inaccurate because the information is considered confidential relative only to the public at large and to nonmembers, but is open to all members. Nothing so confidential that it cannot be disclosed to a buyer's agent should ever be put into the MLS.)

After locating appropriate properties, the buyer's agent should ideally preview them to make sure they fit the desired criteria. Even if it is impractical to inspect all of the properties, a drive-by should be done and the neighborhood surveyed for other properties that may have been missed in the initial search.

SETTING APPOINTMENTS TO SHOW PROPERTY

In MLSs in which it is necessary to call to make an appointment to show a property, you must do two very important things. First, you tell the listing agent, or his or her representative who is setting up the showing, that you are a buyer's agent. (However, in states like Illinois where buyer agency is automatic, this is not necessary.) If your MLS procedure is to make the appointment directly with the seller, you advise the seller of your buyer agency status. In this circumstance, it is also necessary that the listing agent be advised as well. This can be accomplished by a phone call to the listing office or, if the seller isn't home, by leaving a card at the house advising the seller and the listing agent of your status. Second, you should determine the source of your fee.

As most MLSs indicate the buyer agent's fee, your compensation is taken care of automatically. However, if the co-op shown is not sufficient and you intend to ask for additional compensation from either the seller or the buyer, this must be done in the contract to purchase.

When you are making appointments to show unlisted properties, the same two requirements apply. First, you must disclose that you are a buyer's agent and explain what that means. Second, you should ask if there is a selling fee included in the quoted price and, if so, whether it is available to you as a buyer's agent. If the answer to these questions is no and your buyer is unable to pay your fee directly, you must discuss with the seller how your fee will be included in the price; if agreement on this issue cannot be obtained, discuss the situation with your client and advise that you will *not* show this particular property unless you are working *pro bono*. This possibility should have been discussed during the buyer counseling session. Remember that the seller is unrepresented and recommend that he or she obtain advice from an attorney, another real estate broker or both.

SHOWING PROPERTIES

When showing properties to buyer clients, you must be careful about what you say to any owner who may be present during the showing. Reaffirm or remind the seller on first contact that you are the agent of the buyer, as is required by the NAR Code of Ethics, Standard of Practice 16–10. The listing agent should have already taken care of that communication, but sometimes that is not done as it should be. If the seller insists on engaging in conversation, it is acceptable to discuss facts or information about the house or community, and sometimes that can be very helpful. However, be careful about conversations that may violate the confidentiality of the seller, for example, discussions of price or terms or motivation of the seller. These inadvertent slips can alienate a listing agent very quickly, so be careful in these situations.

Just as a side note, in some areas technology has really come of age—so much so that some sellers are apparently wiring their homes to listen to not only what agents are saying about the home but also to listen to any discussion of negotiating techniques discussed by the buyers with their agents. As a result, buyers should be cautioned to be noncommittal in the home (just as they would if the seller were present) and not say anything that they wouldn't want the seller to hear!

In addition to a normal demonstration of the property's benefits and characteristics, you, as a buyer's agent, should also point out deficiencies and defects or even things that in your opinion may detract from the desirability and resalability of the property or affect its value. Unlike buyers' agents, sellers' agents must be careful in this regard, since they must at all times remember that they are the seller's agent and therefore are obligated to promote the seller's best interests. Nonagents must also be careful in this regard because most have the duty not to place one party's interest above those of the other party. Known or obvious defects always must be pointed out by all agents.

Showing homes, especially new homes, often requires buyers' agents to be tech-savvy due to the nationwide trend toward "smart homes" with *structured* wiring: phone and fax lines, pay TV cabling, sound systems, computer connections, Internet capability, security wiring, automated lighting, and more are all in a single, efficient, unified system that can be continually reconfigured to provide updated services. A 2003 survey by the National Association of Home Builders showed that more than 42 percent of new homes include structured wiring, and 78 percent offer it as either a standard or optional feature. A working knowledge of structured wiring and smart home appliances is becoming a mandatory addition to your professional services.

Another tool that's becoming mandatory for top agents is a PDA linked directly to your MLS, allowing you to download details of listings as you and your client drive by for-sale signs. In addition, for as little as $9.99 (RandMcNally StreetFinder) up to $299 (Microsoft's MapPoint 2004), you can load the software equivalent of a GPS-based road atlas into your PDA and never get lost again.

As you show homes, both new and resale, assist your buyer in remembering details about each property by using "showing sheets" with information about each property copied in a way that provides ample adjacent blank space for note taking. If you include more than one property per page, be sure that the information is copied in the order in which the properties will be shown. Sample showing sheets are featured in Figures 9.3 and 9.4. Because looking at a number of properties can be confusing, it is often useful to ask the buyer to play a little game with you. After you have shown the fourth property, ask for a ranking of the four properties and cross off the one the buyer likes least. Continue this process with all remaining showings, so that the buyer never has in mind more than three properties, and these are ranked in order of preference. This will make the final decision process much easier. If you are working with more than one buyer, have both play this game; encourage them to discuss the pros and cons of those properties they especially like. Do not hesitate to give them your opinion from a factual, nonemotional viewpoint.

Remember, if you have really listened during the counseling session and have screened potential properties to determine whether they match the buyer's wants and needs, you should not have to show more than five to ten properties. However, whatever the number of properties you show, continue to listen carefully to your buyers, help them narrow the list to one or two that seem just right, and then ask if they are ready to write a contract.

Your listening skills are your most valuable asset during this stage of the buying process. The following are seven steps from Barbara Ballinger for honing your listening skills: (1) talk *with*, not *at*, your buyers; (2) avoid interrupting; (3) value silence; (4) paraphrase the buyers' comments to ensure your understanding; (5) ask questions; be all ears—or eyes, avoid multitasking; and (6) be honest.

Figure 9.3 / Remember the Homes You Visit

Remember the Homes You Visit
A Checklist

During your search for a home, you'll probably look at several homes. That's a lot to keep track of, especially considering all the pros, cons, and features of each. Use this checklist to track and compare the homes you visit. With this handy record, you'll make fewer revisits and have an easier time determining the best house for you. Besides jotting down notes on each relevant item you may want to rate features and factors on a 10-point scale, with 10 being the best and 0 being nonexistent. If a particular item holds more importance for you, add 4 points. Average your ratings for an overall score.

Address: _____

General		
Feature	**Notes**	**Rating**
Neighborhood/Location		
Curb Appeal/Exterior		
View		
Age of House		
Amount of Natural Light		
Size		
Floor Plan/Traffic Flow		
Interior (note age & condition)		
Flooring		
Wall Color/Coverings		
Cracks, etc.		
Bathrooms		
Water Pressure		
Appliances		
Heat/Air Conditioning		
"Wired" Features*		
Storage		
Kitchen		
Inclusions**		
Exclusions**		
Exterior (note age & condition)		
Gutters (Clean? Covered?)		
Chimney/Fireplace		
Roof		
Garage (Size? Attached?)		
Landscaping/Outdoor seating		
	Overall Rating	

Notes and overall impressions: _____
_____
_____

* High speed data lines, cable connections, jacks, etc.
** Appliances, lighting fixtures, ceiling fans, window treatments, furniture, built-ins, etc.

Figure 9.4 / Taking a 2nd Look?

Taking a 2nd Look?

You'll have a professional inspection should you contract to buy this home. However, now is a good time to look carefully for items you want the inspector to check out in addition to the inspector's standard checklist. Look for cracks, water stains, condition of appliances, etc.

Address: _____

Location	Notes	Sketch
Living Room		
Dining Room		
Kitchen		
Family/Rec Room		
Master Bedroom		
Bedroom 2		
Bedroom 3		
Bedroom 4		
Master Bath		
Bath 2		
Bath 3		
Exterior		
Other		

All of the clever closes in the world will not help if the buyers are not satisfied and ready, so simply ask and they will tell you when they are ready. Remember that your buyer clients are the *only* ones who make the decision. At this stage, your role is to provide assistance and advice.

One last comment about showing property: be careful! Never show property, especially a vacant house, to someone you've never met. This is one of the best reasons for always doing a buyer counseling session. However, even with such a session, follow these precautions: put your police department's phone number on your speed dial, photograph your car and license for your company's records, make a copy of any new prospect's drivers license, and most important, trust your gut instincts.

MAKING THE OFFER

Once the buyer has decided which property to purchase, the real work of the buyer's agent begins. This work consists of guiding the buyer through decisions regarding price, terms, and all other areas of contract negotiations. The role of the buyer's agent, however, differs from that of a seller's agent or nonagent: the guidance of a buyer's agent is true advocacy, advice, and professional opinion. As the contract is brought to closing, the buyer's agent continues to provide guidance by managing the financing, inspections, and other conditions of sale. During this time, the buyer's agent often must forcefully represent the client's interests to the point of additional negotiation.

The Offering Price

Determining what price to offer initially is one of the major decisions a buyer has to make. The buyer's agent should be a big help with this decision because a number of factors affect this determination: the listing price, the real market value of the property, what the buyer can afford to pay, the condition of the property (possible deferred maintenance), and other external factors.

The buyer's agent should perform a complete comparative market analysis (CMA) without any limitation as to the listing price or terms offered. In doing so, point out that the sales prices are what other buyers have paid for a house similar to the one the buyers are looking at in this particular neighborhood. Assist the buyers in determining the differences between the sold properties and the one in question; help them understand whether these differences increase or decrease the value of the property in which they're interested.

On the other hand, a seller's agent or nonagent must be careful in conducting a CMA so as not to violate his or her duty to the seller or, for a nonagent, to act as the buyer's advocate. There are, however, three possible safe methods for agents other than the buyers' agents to use:

1. Perform a complete CMA, and if it supports the listed price, you can present it to the buyer. If, however, it does not support the listed price, it is very risky to give this to the buyer.
2. Ask the listing agent for the CMA used to list the property, and with the seller's permission, he or she may give that to you to show to the buyer. However, if the

listing agent did not prepare a CMA or if it does not justify the listed price, you probably will not have much luck with this approach.

3. If you are a member of an MLS with online computer capability, get a printout of the sales in the entire market area/neighborhood and give it to the buyers, letting them do their own analysis. Because information on properties sold is generally of public record, it probably will not be considered confidential or privileged.

As a buyer's agent, you can and should give advice and express opinions about what you believe the buyers should offer. You can perform any type of evaluation or analysis that you believe is necessary to help your client make a decision. Always remember that the primary objective of buyers is to buy a house that is right for them, not the agent. The buyers make the decision on what to offer and on what terms; you are there to assist the buyers in making the decision, not to make it for them.

The Contract

Because the purchase and sale contract (or contract to buy and sell) is the most important document in the real estate transaction, it must be very carefully prepared. The licensee working either with or for the buyer usually has the responsibility to prepare the initial offer. Remember that there is no contract until both buyer and seller have accepted and signed the offer and have agreed to all terms.

Generally speaking, in most states a statute of frauds requires that contracts for the sale of real property be in writing. There are many other compelling reasons for contracts to be written, so a word to the wise should be sufficient. Put all agreements in writing and never try to conduct a real estate transaction with an oral agreement.

Contracts take many different forms and styles; requirements differ from state to state and, even, association to association. If a standard preprinted form is required, agents have less individual discretion, but all licensees must be aware of what their limits are and when they are exposing themselves to the possibility of the unauthorized practice of law. We will not attempt a full explanation here on contracts or contract law. We will, however, give some suggestions on special considerations in the purchase and sale contract for buyers' agents to assist them in protecting the best interests of their clients, the buyers, and themselves, particularly regarding fees.

Contracts can be one-sided. Here are some ideas that are designed to protect both agent and client. An initial offer tends to favor the party whose representative prepares the document. If standard forms are required by an association or regulatory agency, the offer is more likely to be even-handed. However, additional clauses or provisions are frequently submitted that can change the tenor substantially. You should consider adding provisions that would be beneficial to your client and to you as the buyer's agent.

The buyer needs contractual assurance that all of the items mentioned in Chapter 3 are adequately satisfied, that is, title considerations, property boundaries, inspection of the property (possibly including such things as termite and insect infestation, radon, asbestos, lead-based paint, soil or water

contamination, special districts, etc.), all financing considerations, and the ability to assign the contract. As the buyer's
agent, allow enough time to complete these conditions and
provide adequate safeguards should any condition be unsatisfactory. However, you should caution your buyer client that
loading an offer with extra protective clauses may weaken the
offer, especially in a strong seller's market.

Be sure to make a CLUE report and your buyer's ability to
obtain hazard insurance (see Chapter 8) conditions of the contract. But remember, even an insurance binder is no guarantee: a January 2004 survey of 842 REALTORS® in Colorado
indicated that 10 percent had buyers whose homeowner's
insurance policy was canceled *after* a binder had been issued,
while 15 percent indicated that they had past buyer clients who
were experiencing difficulty renewing their homeowner's
insurance policy because of too many claims from current or
previous owners.

Specific contract provisions for the buyer's agent to consider pertain to agency disclosure and buyer's agent compensation. These items may not be found in standard preprinted
forms, although most states now have mandated disclosure
requirements and preprinted forms.

The agency disclosure is fairly straightforward and merely
states that the selling agent is the agent of the buyer and not
the agent of the seller. Here is some suggested language:

Seller and purchaser hereby acknowledge and agree that
_____ is the Selling Broker and has acted
with respect to this transaction solely as the agent of the
Buyer. Accordingly, Seller acknowledges that, although the
Listing Broker has acted as Seller's agent with respect to

this transaction, no agency relationship exists between Selling Broker and the Seller or Listing Broker. Selling Broker is a fiduciary of the Buyer and *not* the Seller.

The commission or fee provisions can be slightly more complicated because there are three types of fees (retainer, hourly, and success) and three sources of payment (co-op from the listing agent, seller, buyer). A more thorough discussion of the types of fees and the reasons why the fee for the buyer's agent should be included in the sales price is found in Chapter 10. Here we'll consider the sources of the fee because this may need to be included in the purchase and sales agreement, while the type of fee is dealt with in the buyer agency agreement.

In most mature buyer agency markets, buyers' agents receive a co-op fee from the listing agent just as sellers' agents and/or nonagents. If you have confirmed this when you make the appointment to show property, it is not necessary to write anything into the contract regarding a commission split. If, however, the offered co-op is not equal to the fee you've negotiated in the buyer agency contract, or perhaps it's even zero, then it will be necessary to deal with your commission in the contract. There are two choices in this situation: the fee will be paid directly either by the seller or by the buyer. The former is preferable because that method includes the fee in the sales price and therefore in any loan. It should also be remembered that asking the seller to pay the fee of the buyer's agent is really no different than the seller paying any other costs for the buyer, such as discount points or closing or fix-up costs.

However whenever a buyer pays a fee directly, the buyer will usually discount the list price by an amount equal to any other offered co-op fee so that the final amount paid by the buyer is no higher than the original list price. Sample contract language for each of these options follows.

Payment by the seller
This contract is expressly conditional upon Seller crediting Buyer with an amount equal to _____% of the sales price which Buyer agrees to pay to Buyer's Agent as compensation.

Payment by the buyer
Buyer is paying his/her agent's fee directly, outside of closing. As a result, the sales price has been reduced by an amount equal to this fee.

It should be pointed out that prior to 1997, if a buyer's agent received a fee directly from either principal, buyer or seller, this often placed the buyer agent's fee outside the obligation to arbitrate. This was because commissions that could be arbitrated were those wherein there was an agreement between the agents, e.g., any compensation offered in an MLS presumed an agreement between members of that MLS. When total payment of the fee for the buyer's agent came directly from either or both principals, it was presumed that there was no agreement between the agents. This, however, changed with the passage of Standard of Practice 17–4, the effect of which is described in detail in Chapter 12, "Procuring Cause and Arbitration."

Payment of the fee may even be from a combination of these three sources rather than all from one source. Should a buyer's agent be receiving his or her fee from more than one source, this fact must be disclosed. However, it is not necessary to disclose the amount of fee obtained from each source. Just as the buyer's agent has no right to know what the total listing fee negotiated with the seller is, the listing agent has no right to know what the total selling fee is when part comes from a co-op and part comes directly from the buyer's client.

Negotiating the Terms

The negotiation process for the buyer's agent begins when the offer is delivered to the listing agent. The buyer's agent must be a strong advocate for the buyer and should aggressively promote the buyer's position in the offer. If the offer is for less than the listed price, the buyer's agent should be prepared to defend the buyer's offer with comparables and other information that could help influence the seller's decision.

In some markets, the selling agent accompanies the listing agent when the offer is presented. As the buyer's agent, you should insist on the same privilege as a seller's agent or nonagent if this is the custom, because you are better able to represent the buyer's position than is the listing agent. Even if this is not the custom, the standard MLS rules (Section 2.3—Right of Cooperating Broker in Presentation of Offer) allow the buyer's agent to be present. You should do everything possible to present your client's best image and justification for the offer to the seller. Obviously, if the seller is a FSBO, you will be the only agent involved and must present the buyer's offer.

Except in strong buyer's markets, selling new construction homes provides fewer opportunities for negotiation; this should have been discussed with the buyer during the buyer counseling session. Frequently, the base price is effectively fixed, and if any negotiation is possible, it deals with optional items, builder assistance with financing costs, and/or credits to the buyer at closing. However, as the buyer's agent, you should always request that an inspection contingency be included in the purchase contract: just because the builder offers a home warranty is no guarantee that mistakes won't be made during construction.

As negotiation goes back and forth, and the price and terms are changed and modified, it is important to remember that your client (the buyer) still makes the decisions. Sometimes we get so caught up in the transaction and with our desire to obtain the lowest possible price for our buyer client that we forget that the client's real intention is to purchase the property; sometimes, your buyer may be willing to pay more than you think is prudent. Always remember that one of the primary duties of an agent is to obey his or her principal. If the buyer tells you to do something, do it. You can give advice and express your opinion, but never assume that your opinion is the decision of the buyer unless he or she has specifically acknowledged it as such. Do not kill the deal by being too aggressive!

Overall, your negotiating skills will earn you the trust, loyalty, and respect you deserve—plus clients for life. Buyers who are able to reduce the seller's risk of not closing deserve the reward of buying the home for less money and/or on better terms, and of course, the reverse may be true. Therefore, before actually entering into negotiating, it's important to assess your buyer client's strengths and weaknesses.

These strengths and weaknesses begin with the overall market: is it a buyers' or a sellers' market? Next, look at the particular property: Are there many or few appropriate and similar properties in the search area? How long has it been on the market? Have there been other offers? Are any repairs needed? What are the sellers' needs and motivations; what are their goals and objectives? Why is the property being sold? Finally judge your buyer's position: Is the down payment large or small? Are they preapproved or just prequalified for a loan? Do they have any known credit problems? How flexible are they in terms of dates, inclusions and exclusions, and so on?

The basic skills of successful negotiation include your ability to (1) obtain information, (2) negotiate to create a win-win situation, (3) identify the needs versus the wants of the seller, and (4) not take the negotiating process personally. Apply the 80:20 rule of negotiation: invest 80 percent of your time getting information by listening, learning, and analyzing the needs of your buyer client and the seller; use the remaining 20 percent of the time giving appropriate information to the parties involved in the negotiation.

A few more tips can be useful to the skilled buyer's agent. Remember that most concessions are made at the very end of a negotiation, so be patient. Deadlines are often more flexible than people realize: try to learn the other side's deadline— without revealing yours. Finally, remain calm.

In summary, the true power in negotiating comes from knowledge and knowledge comes from information. Your role as the buyer's agent is to use your information and knowledge to create a negotiating strategy that tilts the scales towards your buyer client.

Managing the Closing Process

The entire process of closing the transaction begins as soon as the contract is fully executed. Many conditions need to be met, and most of them are the buyer's responsibility. If they are the buyer's responsibility, that means the buyer's agent must be closely involved in seeing that they are done. Let's take a look at some of the items that need to be addressed.

- A complete chronological list of all the performance dates. This would include all of the contingency requirements and performance dates for accomplishing any requirement of the contract. Providing the buyer with a calendar showing the dates is an excellent visual aid.
- A careful analysis of all of the contingencies to determine who will assist with each one. Financing, all inspections, survey, and any other due diligence will usually be the responsibility of the buyer and his or her agent. The listing agent will normally take care of depositing the earnest money, arranging for the closing process or opening escrow, ordering the title commitment or obtaining the abstract, and generally helping with access to the property when necessary. Good communication between all the parties is extremely important at this stage.
- Recommendation of reliable sources for all of the buyer's needs. Out-of-town or first-time buyers especially will not usually have ready sources for financing, inspection, surveying, or even legal services, for that matter, and the buyer's agent must be prepared to make appropriate suggestions. It is a good idea to recommend more than one source and give the buyer a choice of people who you know can be relied upon to do good work. Make sure that you do not recommend any source that you have not had satisfactory service from in the past or who has not been referred to you by a very reliable informant.

- Helping the buyer through these due diligence requirements. Once again, an unsophisticated or first-time
  buyer will need help, particularly with the complications of financing and probably with the inspections.
  Any complications or deficiencies found will need to be
  documented and reported to the listing agent or seller
  for proper disposition. The buyer's agent can be most
  helpful in this phase, since it may require some additional negotiation on the buyer's behalf.

- Assistance with the closing or settlement activity. A
  buyer who has never participated in the closing of a real
  estate transaction can find the experience very confusing and threatening. A good agent provides aid and
  comfort at this time. As the buyer's agent, you must
  have a thorough knowledge of the settlement process,
  regardless of the competence of the closer, since your
  client will look to you for advice and assurance that
  everything is all right. If you have done a thorough job
  in the counseling session, the closing process will go
  more smoothly.

CLOSING GIFTS

Closing gifts are more than just an unexpected courtesy;
they serve as a sincere show of appreciation for business and a
low-key way to generate referrals. Many top agents are coming
to see that there actually are two "closings" in a real estate
transaction—one that occurs in a blizzard of paperwork at the
settlement table and a more friendly one that occurs shortly
thereafter when the agent delivers a gift sealing his or her rela-

tionship with the client. In addition to a gift, we always include a copy of our "Recommended Vendors" list, asking the buyer/ new owner to let us know of any names that should be added as well as any names that should be removed due to poor service. This second closing is an excellent springboard to referrals and repeat business in the future.

Here is a list of gifts that will be remembered as opposed to the "usual" flowers and champagne:

- reverse osmosis water filter that fits on the kitchen sink;
- homeowner's record book for organizing important home-related documents as well as all home improvement receipts;
- amateur do-it-yourself kit (especially for first-time buyers);
- nicely framed, artistic rendering of the home and/or note cards made from the painting;
- new locks for all doors and windows;
- baseball bats personalized with a child's name from the Louisville Slugger bat manufacturing plant in Louisville, Kentucky;
- tree-cuttings from trees that are directly linked to U.S. history (old trees that stood guard at the signing of the Declaration of Independence and/or, adorned the homes of presidents, poets, and inventors) can be obtained from American Forests Historic Tree Nursery (*www.historictrees.org*).

Gifts today can reflect the professionalism of the giver, the personality of the receiver, or even the spirit of a transaction that has evolved into a friendship. A NAR Information Survey conducted in April 2003 found 77 percent of REALTORS® gave closing gifts, spending and average of $54.20 per closing. In 2002, REALTORS® gave an estimated 12 million closing gifts valued at a total of $646 million.

SUMMARY

Locating properties to show can be much more intensive for you as buyer's agent than for a seller's agent or nonagent because the entire market is available. Although you will probably look first at MLS-listed properties including company listings, you should go beyond that to FSBOs, bank foreclosures, and even to properties for which there is no indication that their owners are interested in selling.

Although buyers' agents in the past had some problems in establishing their credibility and rights to participate fully in the traditional MLS system, most of this resistance has disappeared, and buyers' agents today function in the same way as other licensees. MLS rules should allow free access to listed properties, cooperation, and fair compensation. If they do not, appropriate "political" action should be taken to change that policy.

As a buyer's agent, you will need to exercise extra care in the showing of properties by providing buyers with information about any deficiencies that might affect resalability as well as defects. Be sure to disclose your status to both listing agents and sellers. If your behavior is appropriate, you will have much more latitude and flexibility in truly representing the client as a buyer's agent than as a seller's agent or nonagent.

It is in the offering, negotiating, and closing phases of the transaction that you will really earn your compensation. Your effectiveness as an advocate and negotiator on the buyer's behalf is the true determinant of your success as a buyer's agent. A seller's agent or nonagent will be involved in most of the activities mentioned but must be very careful not to become too aggressive on the buyer's behalf, letting others believe he or she is the buyer's advocate, thus inadvertently becoming an undisclosed dual agent. A buyer's agent is subject to no such restraint.

A well-written contract that clearly expresses the intentions of the parties is vital to the success of the transaction. A professional buyer's agent will see to it that the buyer's interests are well represented during the initial negotiation of the contract as well as during the time between contract and closing.

Closing gifts today are the icing on the cake that helps convert the buyer's memory of your professionalism during the transaction to a client-for-life relationship.

REVIEW QUESTIONS

1. Listing agents can legally give buyers a CMA indicating a value
   a. less than list price.
   b. equal to list price.
   c. Neither
   d. Both

ANSWER:

b. If a listing agent provided a buyer customer with a CMA showing a value less than the list price, that would be a conflict of interest since as listing agent he or she had a duty to get the seller the highest price. A listing agent can, of course, provide a CMA indicating a value equal to or greater than list price.

2. A buyer agent's potential inventory of properties includes
   a. FSBOs.
   b. MLS listings.
   c. in-house listings.
   d. unlisted properties.
   e. All of the above

ANSWER:

d. Buyers' agents should show buyers all properties that meet the buyers' requirements including not only MLS listings but unlisted properties as well, such as FSBOs, repossessed properties, properties with no indication that the owner might want to sell, and listings from other companies that are not on the MLS.

3. The biggest potential liability exposure when selling an unlisted property is
   a. determining the value.
   b. deciding how you will be paid.
   c. working with an unrepresented seller.
   d. None of the above

ANSWER:

c. A buyer's agent should have little or no problem determining the value of a property or negotiating how to be paid.
However, there are pitfalls in working with an unrepresented
seller as assistance and communication can be interpreted as
representation and thus undisclosed dual agency.

4. As a buyer's agent which of the following can you do when
   showing properties that a nonagent or listing agent cannot
   do?
   a. Give your opinion and advice about all the defects and
      deficiencies in the property
   b. Explain the zoning
   c. Discuss the restrictive covenants
   d. Point out schools and shopping

ANSWER:

a. Choices (b), (c), and (d) are all information that an agent
can and should provide to both client and customer. The same is
true of any material defects. However, deficiencies (e.g., only
one bath and it's off the kitchen; the street is quiet now, but you
may want to revisit during "rush" hour) should only be disclosed
to a buyer client as these may reduce the value of the property
relative to its list price and make it more difficult to resell.

CHAPTER 10

Compensation

Compensation is the most misunderstood and frequently the most controversial issue in the real estate business. It is the source of most disputes and has created many false impressions in the mind of the public about the professionalism and integrity of real estate licensees. In the beginning (1980s–1990s), confusion about compensation of buyers' agents was even more pronounced, primarily because the practice was new and also because it changed some long-standing traditions that many in the business did not want to see changed.

The public often perceives a real estate broker or salesperson as being extremely wealthy, the owner of a Cadillac or Mercedes Benz loaded with high tech equipment. Although many top producers fit this image, the vast majority of licensees make an average living, and the attrition rate is very, very high.

One factor that has helped create this sometimes negative image has been our reluctance to discuss our fees in an open and forthright manner. With the trends of disclosure and agency awareness, it is becoming more and more important to hold frank and open discussions about how, when, and how much we expect to be paid for our services. We must not keep any secrets from our clients, whether they are buyers or sellers.

SOURCE OF COMMISSION DOES NOT DETERMINE AGENCY

For many years, it was believed that whoever paid your fee was your principal and that merely paying a fee created an agency relationship. This is simply not true and, according to most common law, has never been true. In an 1881 decision (*Bell v. McConnell*, 37 Ohio St. 305, 41 Am. Rep. 528) the Supreme Court of Ohio stated, in effect, that compensation can come from any source, provided that there is disclosure and consent of all parties. Almost every state has a statute, legal precedent, or regulation that says basically the same thing. The payment of a commission can be one factor used in the determination of agency, but it is rarely, if ever, the only consideration.

Buyers' agents can receive compensation from a variety of sources including the buyer, the seller, both buyer and seller, or most commonly, the listing broker. They can participate in the ownership of property and can donate or forgo a commission. In essence, buyers' agents can do anything they desire for their consideration, provided that it is disclosed and consented to by their principal, the buyer. It may also be necessary to disclose the fact of a commission but not its amount to the seller, the listing agent, or a third party who is a material part of the arrangement. It is not necessary, however, to disclose a confidential agreement between buyers' agents and their principals if the other parties are not affected in any way. The same is true of listing agents and sellers, because the terms of the total listing fee are confidential and do not necessarily reflect any co-op or buyer's agent compensation.

There are two important key issues that could determine whether or not a buyer's agent is even entitled to receive a commission on a specific transaction. These two issues deal with *abandonment* and *estrangement.*

Abandonment occurs when the broker simply disengages from the transaction or fails to communicate with the client.

Estrangement is similar to abandonment, but results when the buyer terminates the relationship because of the agent's conduct. For example, if the buyer lives out of town and the agent has made no provision for accomodating the buyer, this could be a situation that may lead to estrangement; or if the broker takes a vacation or has to leave town for some reason and is not available to serve the client, this would also be a situation that could lead to estrangement.

AVOID A CONFLICT OF INTEREST

It is critical to avoid even the possible perception of a conflict of interest. In all aspects of the negotiation process involving payment of fees, you must be careful not to allow the payment of additional or special consideration by the other party to the contract to create an obligation to that party that could be considered a conflict of interest. Your behavior after the fact is very important lest your client suspect that your loyalty has wavered or changed in the slightest.

Sometimes a conflict of interest is hard to discern, particularly for real estate salespeople and brokers. For so long, we have been primarily "deal makers," working frequently for both parties to a transaction and looking out for the best interests of both sides. Now that we are agents, we must be particularly careful if we receive something of beneficial value or even the promise of something in the future (such as a future listing or sale) from someone *other* than our client.

CONTINGENT VERSUS NONCONTINGENT FEES

Contingent fees, those received only upon a successful closing, compose the vast majority of the fees received by real estate agents. As a result, most agents have had the frustrating experience of doing a lot of work for either a buyer or a seller and never getting paid because the transaction did not close.

The concept of noncontingent fees, which is becoming more prevalent in our industry, is quite popular with buyers' agents. As we establish ourselves as true professionals, noncontingent fees will become more common, as we learn to value our time much more. We realize that it is our only resource and we cannot continue to give it away. Other professionals such as lawyers and accountants have always charged for their time; now it is time we start thinking the same way.

The noncontingent fee can be an hourly charge for the time spent, which is billed on a current basis. It can also be a fixed fee for performing a specified task that may or may not result in closing a real estate transaction. Sometimes the fee earned is credited against a commission or success fee to create more incentive. Whatever the formula, the principle is that we be compensated for the time we spend on behalf of our client, no matter what the outcome of the assignment.

Generally speaking, it takes a highly experienced salesperson or broker to be able to command noncontingent fees, but many practitioners fall into this category. As we become busier and more successful, we get more and more conscious of the value of our time. This fee option is certainly worth consideration.

RETAINER FEES

One popular method for determining at least a part of the compensation for buyers' agents is the retainer fee. For most homebuyers, this would not be a large amount, probably somewhere in the $500 range, but it does give the buyer an incentive to perform the contract and finalize the purchase. However, a retainer fee should not be used to "buy" the buyer's loyalty, because that seems to negate the relationship of trust and respect you've initially established during the buyer counseling session and maintained by your behavior throughout the transaction. The buyer agency contract is all the loyalty you need because payment of your fee due under the terms of that contract can, if necessary, be enforced in court.

The retainer fee can be either nonrefundable or, in some cases, refundable. It can be credited against the success fee or commission, much the same as the hourly fees, or it can be refunded after a short time and with few hours spent if some specified factor prevents the buyer from proceeding with a purchase (e.g., not being able to prequalify for a loan). Be sure to check local and state regulations concerning retainer fees, because in some states, including California, retainer fees must be deposited in a broker's trust account.

Table 10.1 / Hourly Fee Calculation

Desired Annual Salary	Divided	Hourly Salary	Overhead Multiple	Total Hourly Fee
$25,000	by 1,800 working hours/ year	$14/hr.	3 (Overhead + Nonproductive Time)	$42/hr. (Value of time chargeable to client)
$50,000		$28/hr.	3	$83/hr.
$100,000		$56/hr.	3	$167/hr.

SETTING THE FEE

There are a number of different methods for determining the fee of a buyer's agent.

Hourly Fee

If an hourly fee is charged, it will be set, at least in part, on what the market will bear, and the amount will vary substantially from market to market. It could be compared to what other professionals such as lawyers and accountants receive and should be graduated on the basis of your experience and qualifications. One word of advice: do not underestimate your value. If you price yourself too cheaply, your client may not believe you are as good as you really are. See Table 10.1 for a suggested formula for setting an hourly fee. Eighteen hundred hours is the average number of working hours per year as established by those who study work. This is merely a suggested formula to use as a guide.

Fixed (Flat) Fee

You may wish to calculate a straight fixed fee that does not vary with final sales price. This can be roughly equivalent to the average selling percentage for a house in the buyer's desired price range. If the buyer suggests a wide price range, you can take the average of the range multiplied by the percentage. The agreement can include some provision for an adjustment if the price of the house the buyer purchases is substantially higher or lower than the original price range. This could happen if the buyer initially wanted to buy at a substantially lower price than he or she could afford, and then reconsidered after starting to look at homes. Once the fee is agreed on, it can be paid either by the buyer or as a co-op fee by the listing broker or seller. If the co-op fee is less than the agreed-on fixed fee, the buyer would have to make up the difference. If the co-op fee is more, the buyer's agent could rebate the difference to the buyer client.

Percentage Fee

This is usually simply a percentage of the sales price or the offered co-op fee in the MLS. The problem with the straight percentage is that it creates a disincentive for the buyer's agent to get a lower price for the buyer, since a higher price generates a higher fee for the buyer's agent. As a result, most percentage fees create a conflict of interest that must be discussed with the buyer client. As with any conflict of interest, the only way to deal with it is to disclose its existence and then determine a solution acceptable to both you and your client. There are four possible solutions:

1. The flat fee
2. A fee based on the list price rather than the sales price
3. A bonus incentive based on a percentage of the difference between the list and sales prices combined with a relatively low percentage success fee
4. Acceptance of the co-op fee following a conversation designed to place the conflict in perspective

Our experience is that the last is the most effective solution, because the other three all require credit and debit adjustments when the fee negotiated is different from the co-op fee offered.

Such a conversation could be something like the following. "Let's try to put this conflict we've just identified into perspective. We've just agreed that you'll pay me a fee of 3 percent (this is used only for example because fees vary substantially). Because you're in the $100,000 range. If you paid full price, that would be a fee of $3,000. Now, in our marketplace, the average list-to-sales-price ratio is 98.5, which means, on average, you'd pay $98,500 for that $100,000 listing. Let's say that I could negotiate a really good deal for you, say 95 percent of list price or $95,000; at 3 percent, my fee would be $2,850. What's the difference between that and my fee at full price?" The buyer usually will say, "Why, that's only $150!" At this point you say, "Yes, and I can't be bought for $150!" When they ask what you mean, explain that your business is a referral business that depends on repeat business and client referrals. Ask, "Would you come back to me for future real estate business or refer your friends and relatives to me if you didn't think that I'd done a really good job for you?" The answer, of course, is no, at which point you say, "Of course not, and I won't jeopardize future business from you by maximizing my commission today to the detriment of your interest in getting the lowest price possible."

There are two outcomes from this simple conversation: (1) You put your commission in perspective (i.e., it changes very little with sales price negotiations for any particular property) and (2) you've asked for future business in a way that's memorable because you've tied it to money.

PAYING THE FEE

The fee of the buyer's agent should be included in the sales price for the following reasons:

- Reliability of comparables: If the fee of the buyer's agent is not included in the sales price, it will give an erroneous price for comparable sales. There is usually no method to rectify this situation.
- Accuracy of assessed valuations: Assessors will usually rely on recorded sales prices as one of the factors to fix assessed values, and these will be inaccurate for the reason cited above.
- Maximizing loan amounts: The maximum loan available to a buyer is usually a percentage of the sales price. Accordingly, including all sale commissions and fees in the sales price increases the upper limit of the amount of an available loan. This argument assumes that the buyer will use a portion of the down payment to pay his or her agent directly. Therefore, the amount of loan he or she can obtain is reduced by the loan-to-value ratio times the commission amount. For example, on a $3,000 commission and an 80 percent loan, the possible

down payment would be reduced by $3,000, which, when divided by 20 percent (the down payment percentage), results in a $15,000 lower loan amount. This can be a substantial penalty for the buyer.

■ Commission as a component of value: Traditionally, real estate commissions have been included in the sales price. This practice has been justified on the basis that real estate agents provide a valuable service and that this service is a normal cost of the transaction. However, if the commission of the listing broker is included in the sales price but the fee of the buyer's agent is not, industry detractors and consumer advocates may use that as a basis for questioning the inclusion of any sales commission in a transaction.

If the buyer's agent's fees are considered in the same context as all other commissions, that is, as a cost of the transaction, then transactions in which both buyer and seller are represented can be conducted with very little disruption. There should be no additional cost to anyone involved, provided all parties act in a fair and reasonable manner.

SUMMARY

As can be seen by now, the topic of compensation is not only one of the most important but also one of the most misunderstood and controversial topics.

Many different methods of compensation are available to the buyer's agent; it is important to choose the ones that work for your particular practice and clientele. There are also many compelling reasons to include the fee for the buyer's agent in the sales price of the property. It is important to accomplish this with as little impact on the buyer as possible, since frequently buyers with limited cash may have difficulty paying their agent directly. Unless some accommodation is made, the buyer's ability to complete the transaction may be impaired.

Generally, buyers' agents are compensated by the seller as a cost of the transaction. Sellers are usually quite willing to do so, provided that the compensation does not increase the amount already agreed to in the listing contract. It is important to work cooperatively with listing agents to accommodate what is best for both principals, buyer and seller. Today virtually all listing brokers cooperate in this process, because they realize that it is in their sellers' best interests.

REVIEW QUESTIONS

1. The commission for the buyer's agent can come from which of the following sources?
   a. The buyer directly
   b. The seller directly as a co-op fee
   c. The seller's agent as part of the fee paid to him
   d. All of the above

ANSWER:

   d. A buyer's agent can be paid from any source provided he or she discloses the source(s) to all parties to the contract.

2. If the fee for the buyer's agent is not included as part of the sales price, the recorded price, relative to other compara-ble properties, will be
   a. too low.
   b. too high.

ANSWER:

   a. If a buyer's agent fee is not included in the sales price, then the sales price will be lower by that commission amount; the affected property will not be a good comparable.

3. The most common situations that create a questionable right to receive a commission are
   a. abandonment.
   b. estrangement.
   c. Both
   d. Neither

ANSWER:

   c. Abandonment and estrangement are the two primary reasons that a hearing panel might use to question an agent's right to receive a commission even if the agent has a buyer agency contract.

4. Abandonment occurs under which of the following circum-stances?
   a. When the broker disengages from the transaction
   b. When the broker fails to communicate with the client
   c. Both
   d. Neither

ANSWER:

c. Poor, or lack of, communication by the agent and/or noninvolvement of the agent with the buyer client are the facts that will lead a hearing panel to find that the agent has abandoned the client.

CASE STUDY:
A Change in Offered Compensation

Frank Smith listed Linda Maxwell's home and filed the listing with the MLS. The property data sheet indicated the compensation Frank was offering to the other participants if they were successful in finding a buyer for Linda's home.

During the next few weeks, several agents, including Suzie, showed Linda's home to potential buyers. Although several showings were made, no offers to purchase were forthcoming. Frank and Linda, in discussing possible means of making the property more salable, agreed to reduce the listed price. Frank also agreed to lower his commission. Frank changed his compensation offer in the MLS and then called the agents who had shown Linda's property to advise them that he was modifying his offer of compensation to cooperating brokers. Upon receiving the call, Suzie responded that she was working with Jim who appeared to be very interested in purchasing the property and who would probably make an offer to purchase in the next day or two. Suzie indicated that she would expect to receive the compensation that had been published originally in the MLS and not the reduced amount now being offered to her, since she had already shown the property to Jim and expected an offer to purchase would be made shortly. Frank responded that since Jim had not signed an offer to purchase, the modified offer of compensation would be applicable.

The following day, Suzie wrote an offer to purchase for Jim. The offer was submitted to the seller by Frank and was accepted. At the closing, Frank gave Suzie a check for services in an amount reflecting the modified offer communicated to Suzie by phone. Suzie refused to accept the check indicating that she felt Frank's actions were in violation of the Code of Ethics. Suzie filed a complaint with the Board's Grievance Committee.

During the hearing, Suzie stated that Frank's modification of the compensation constituted a misrepresentation through concealment of pertinent facts since he had not provided Suzie with specific written notification of the modification prior to the time Suzie began her efforts to interest the purchaser in the listed property. Frank defended his actions by indicating that timely notice of the modification of compensation offered had been provided to Suzie by telephone prior to Suzie obtaining a signed offer to purchase. Frank also indicated that his modified offer of compensation had been bulletined to all agents who had shown the property. Frank also commented that had Suzie produced the signed offer to purchase prior to Frank communicating the modified offer, then Frank would have willingly paid the amount originally offered.

    a.   Should Frank have done anything differently?

    b.   Who was right, Frank or Suzie?

ANSWERS:

    a.   Frank was correct in immediately telephoning all the agents who had shown Linda's house and telling them about both the price and commission change. It would have been even better if he had sent both a written letter and e-mail.

b. Frank was right because his disclosure was made before Suzie wrote her contract, thus giving Suzie enough time to discuss the price and commission changes with Jim. Suzie should have covered this possibility in her buyer agency contract with Jim.

CASE STUDY:
Variable Commission Rate

Aaron North and Nanette South were members of the same board and participants in the multiple-listing service. Aaron, cooperating with Nanette on Nanette's listing, presented an offer to purchase signed by buyers offering the listed price, and a check for earnest money. The only contingency was a mortgage contingency, and Aaron shared with Nanette qualifying information about the buyers indicating there should be no problem securing a mortgage. The following day, Nanette returned the offer to Aaron with "REJECTED" written on it and initialed by the seller, and explained that the seller had accepted another offer secured by one of Nanette's sales associates. Aaron inquired about the seller's reason for rejecting the full price offer with only a mortgage contingency, and what had caused the seller to accept the other offer. Nanette responded that she did not know, but with equal offers, she supposed the seller would favor the offer secured by the listing broker.

Later, Aaron met the seller at a social event. The seller thanked him for his efforts in connection with the recent sale of the seller's home. The seller hoped Aaron understood there was nothing personal in his decision, adding that the money he saved through his special agreement with Nanette had been the deciding factor. When Aaron asked about the "special agreement," the seller explained he had signed a listing agreement for the sale of his property that authorized the submission of the listing to the multiple-listing service and specified a certain amount of compensation. However, the seller stated that he had also signed an addendum to the listing agreement specifying that if Nanette sold the listing through her own office, a percentage of the agreed compensation would be discounted to the seller's credit, resulting in a lower commission payable by the seller.

    a.   Should the variable commission have been disclosed to Aaron?

    b.   Is a variable commission a material fact?

ANSWERS:

    a. Variable commissions should always be disclosed to potential selling/buyer agents so that the buyer can determine how to make a competitive offer. Failing to disclose the actual terms and conditions of the compensation offered through the MLS results in concealment and misrepresentation of pertinent facts to both the selling/buyer agent and to the buyer.

    b. Yes, a variable commission is a material fact because knowledge of it can make a difference to the buyer and his or her agent.

11

Special Commercial Applications

Because of some unique characteristics of commercial real estate, it is important to discuss a few of the aspects of agency, and particularly buyer agency, as they relate to it. Commercial transactions are often more complicated, generally take much longer to complete, and may involve more repeat clients than residential transactions. Thus, in the past, buyer and tenant agency has been more commonplace in the commercial area than in the residential specialties.

Commercial agents use various approaches to the disclosure regulations. Some practice disclosure and others do not address it at all. Some disclose to buyers only and not tenants. Some states exclude commercial agents from agency disclosure requirements. The fact remains, however, that as far as common law is concerned, commercial transactions have the same legal ramifications as residential transactions. With that in mind, we will look briefly at leasing, exchanges, and vacant ground, all of which differ in some respects from the more usual purchase of residential property.

There are, because of the wide variety of properties, many other special considerations in commercial real estate, many of which will require much more investigation and research (due diligence) for the buyer. However, most of the same principles and procedures apply for both commercial and residential buyers' agents. If commercial agents ignore the agency requirements and responsibilities, they expose themselves to the same potential liability as any other agent, except that the stakes are often much higher and the potential losses much greater.

LEASING

For many years, leasing was a function of the management of the property and was included in the duties of the property manager. However, beginning in the 1970s, leasing has become a specialty of its own and has become very big business, particularly in large metropolitan areas. As the leasing specialty matured, it developed some habits and practices that now must be adjusted to compensate for the requirements of agency law.

For many years, leasing agents have supposedly been "representing" tenants by showing them potential properties, registering them with the listing agent or owner's representative, and then withdrawing from the transaction, hoping to receive a fee when the transaction is complete. The procedures vary from market to market, but generally are rather loose and not consistently enforced. The problem with this method was that tenants were left with no negotiating help and generally at the mercy of the landlord's agent, unless they were represented by their own lawyer.

Under this scenario, agency was not a consideration, and most of the "representation" letters signed by tenants really did not address the question of agency. Landlords paid the leasing commissions because they were a cost of the operation of the property and were built into the budget. The system seemed to work and, to a large extent, still operates in the same way except in areas where agency has become an important consideration. The changes that have occurred are prompted by disclosure requirements or simply by agents who realize the faults of the traditional system and want to truly represent tenants.

Because there is no purchase and sale contract that specifies performance dates and requirements, the leasing process does not readily accommodate the issues of agency disclosure and agent compensation. These matters must be handled in separate documentation. The tenant representation agreement or tenant agency contract should be very similar to the buyer agency contract and can be adapted from that format. Any agreement, whether it is a representation agreement or an agency contract, must have a clear statement of the agency relationships as well as the other important elements, such as the term of the agreement, the type of premises desired, and compensation arrangements. Basically, if you are to protect your fee, this agreement should contain enough information to leave no doubt as to your exact relationship with the tenant. Tenant Representation or TenRep has become very popular and is considered a category all its own in commercial real estate.

If you are acting as a tenant's agent, the relationship must be disclosed to the listing agent and landlord, just as is true of buyer agency. You must also clearly establish how you will be paid, so that there is no question about this matter later on, after it is too late to establish your position. All of these items should be in written agreements approved by your attorney, because most jurisdictions do not have standard forms for them. This also can be easily accommodated as part of a lease proposal or letter of intent, which would include the agency disclosure and fee arrangements as well as some performance dates.

As a tenant's agent, you can freely work on your client's behalf by assisting in the negotiation, performing analyses of different properties, making recommendations, and giving advice. As simply a registered agent, you must be careful how you act, and most likely you will have to stay completely out of the negotiation process. We are seeing some companies formed strictly to represent tenants as agents, and many of these are having success with tenants paying the fees. With buyer agency, this concept is likely to become more common in the commercial market as well.

One of the more common causes of a dispute occurs when a tenant exercises the legal right to representation and hires an agent who expects to be compensated by the landlord. Unfortunately, this frequently involves tenants who wish to remain in their present building but want help negotiating the new lease. The solution for this dilemma is for the landlord to clearly state his or her policy for agent fees in the lease itself. This can help avoid serious disputes and also possibly save some tenants who might vacate if they cannot have proper representation along with payment of their agent.

EXCHANGES

Most exchangers probably have given little thought to the question of agency, although it is now an important consideration with the advent of disclosure. Dual agency has always been an element of like-kind exchanges, but it was not usually a problem because one agent represented one side and another agent, the other side. The problem arose when each agent was also considered a subagent for the property his or her client was purchasing.

A solution for this dilemma would be to have a buyer agency agreement signed at the same time you get the listing signed and then merely include the proper disclosures in the exchange contract. This procedure could help prevent the dual agency complications from arising at a later date. Experienced exchangers should not have a problem with this, because it is just a precautionary step that makes common sense.

Agency agreements are particularly important if each side is represented by a different agent of the same broker, because this would require a company policy of dual agency/designated brokerage/nonagency for in-house sales (see Chapter 5) and a signed in-house sale amendment for both the listing and the buyer agency contract. Obviously, the disclosure requirement becomes even more critical when one agent represents more than one party to the exchange. The practice of "pooling and splitting fees" intensifies the dual agency aspect of an exchange and is not recommended. As a result, most exchangers today use the YKY–IKM (you keep yours–I keep mine) formula.

VACANT GROUND

There are a number of circumstances in which buyer agency can be very advantageous for buyers of vacant ground or building sites. Buyers' agents can be especially helpful to users who are looking for parcels on which to build a facility, as well as to chains or franchises, commercial or residential developers, and land speculators. Buyers' agents can spend time and effort searching for all the possibilities and not be limited to listed properties or properties that are already on the market. Frequently, buyers for these properties require a lot of research and analysis; the experienced buyer's agent who negotiates such an arrangement ensures that he or she will be compensated for those efforts.

Another big opportunity lies in the assemblage of parcels of land for speculators or developers. It is usually critical for these purchasers to maintain anonymity, and only the buyer's agent can legally and successfully operate in this manner. Frequently, the buyer's agent will act as a nominee for the purchaser, do the transaction in his or her name, and be compensated totally by the client.

Vacant ground brokerage also allows some unique opportunities for the buyer agent to be compensated with some future "upside" in addition to current fees. Buyer agents can become joint venture partners in future development or partners in land syndications. Fees can be taken as a portion of the profit in any future sale, or the agent can be given a piece of the property as compensation. By and large, the only practical way to accommodate these types of compensation is through an agency relationship with the purchasing entity.

SUMMARY

Commercial real estate agents have many opportunities to use buyer agency as a sales tool for increasing business. The problem lies in the fact that agents often do not want to experiment with something they think is new. In reality, buyer agency is not new to the commercial market; it has been used for a long time, but it has not been recognized as such.

The leasing business needs the most attention and also offers the greatest opportunity. Leasing agents must recognize agency relationships and responsibilities and do the proper disclosure and documentation. Some minimal attention to details can prevent the loss of commissions and the waste of a lot of time and effort. Tenants' representatives or tenreps can find a whole new market and clientele by selling their services as true negotiators and representatives of tenants in the leasing process.

Exchanges, by their very nature, present numerous opportunities for agency complexities. The buyer's agent who represents clients in an exchange must do so with great care.

Undeveloped ground for site selection, development, or speculation presents many opportunities for the buyer's agent, and the possibilities for reward are tremendous. Buyers' agents have much more latitude and flexibility in searching the marketplace, and sophisticated purchasers look for that kind of representation.

REVIEW QUESTIONS

1. Which is not one of the five basic types of commercial real estate properties in today's market?
   a. Office buildings
   b. Shopping centers
   c. Industrial properties
   d. Vacant ground for development
   e. Multifamily residential properties
   f. Single-family residential

ANSWER:

    f. Items (a)–(e) are all commercial specialties; the sale of single-family homes is a residential specialty.

2. Commercial brokers do which of the following functions?
   a. Sales to users
   b. Leases
   c. Exchanges
   d. Sales to investors
   e. All of the above

ANSWER:

    e. Items (a)–(d) are all functions of commercial brokers.

3. Regarding the commercial property types listed in Question 1 above,
   a. all have identical types of actual practice.
   b. each is a unique specialty.
   c. all are usually listed and sold by residential brokers.
   d. they can only be listed and sold by commercial brokers.

ANSWER:

b.   Unlike residential properties, commercial property types each require slightly different to substantially different practices because each is a unique specialty. As specialties, they are rarely practiced by residential brokers; however, it would be entirely legal for a residential broker to list and/or sell commercial properties. Such practice is not limited to commercial brokers and it is not uncommon for a residential broker to occasionally list/sell a commercial property.

4. Commercial transactions are
   a. subject to the same disclosure requirements as residential transactions.
   b. subject to different disclosure requirements than residential transactions.
   c. subject to caveat emptor.

ANSWER:

a.   Commercial transactions are based on real estate just like residential transactions. Therefore they are subject to the same disclosure requirements. Except in a very few states, this includes full disclosure of all material facts, and therefore, caveat emptor does not apply.

5. The duties of a tenant's agent are
   a. the same as for a buyer's agent.
   b. different from a buyer's agent.
   c. not important because lawyers are always involved

ANSWER:

a. A tenant's agent or tenant's rep has the same agency duties as a buyer's agent. The difference is that a tenant's agent assists tenants in leasing offices and other types of commercial property. The fact that a lawyer may also represent the tenant does not change the tenant rep's duties.

12

Procuring Cause and Arbitration

Procuring cause has been one of the most misunderstood concepts in relation to buyer agency. Guidelines approved in November 1996 clean up many of the inconsistencies regarding buyer agency. There is still a tendency, however, for many long-time practitioners and, consequently, many hearing panels, to give too much weight to the old procuring cause theory of the "threshold rule." There is also confusion, especially in the minds of some exclusive buyers' agents, regarding buyer agency contract and procuring cause. The former does not necessarily result in the latter.

HISTORICAL PERSPECTIVE

In the days of *caveat emptor,* the procuring cause guideline was simply the *threshold rule.* This meant that the person who initially showed the property to the eventual buyer received the selling commission. This rule was practically absolute, and no questions were asked about who actually sold the property, prepared the contract, and closed the transaction. This guideline and rule operated from the late 1970s to the 1980s and still prevails today in some isolated cases or with unenlightened associations and licensees.

In 1993, NAR expanded its procuring cause guidelines from the original 10 to 32. However, these extensive guidelines created some confusion for hearing panels, and a Procuring Cause Working Group was appointed in 1995 to better organize the approach to procuring cause. The guidelines resulting from this group's work were passed in November 1996, and are broken down into six recommended factors for consideration by hearing panels. They are offered as a guide to panels to aid them in reaching fair and logical decisions. The six factors are:

1. no predetermined rule of entitlement;
2. arbitrability and appropriate parties;
3. relevance and admissibility;
4. communication and contact—abandonment and estrangement;
5. conformity with state law; and
6. consideration of the entire course of events.

Communication looks at the frequency and type of communication used by the broker and contact looks at timing and methods of and benefits of contact to the client. Abandonment occurs with the broker's inactivity or disengagement from the transaction. Estrangement occurs when the broker's conduct or failure to act causes the buyer client to end the relationship.

Additionally, this list of factors is accompanied by a detailed series of questions that are representative of those commonly involved in arbitration hearings. These questions cover the nature, status, and terms of the transaction, listing agreement, and compensation offer. They also address the roles, relationship, and conduct of the parties involved in the transaction, the continuity of the transaction, as well as issues related to leasing transactions.

A broker will be regarded as the **procuring cause** of a sale, so as to be entitled to commission , if his or her efforts are the foundation on which the negotiations resulting in a sale are begun. A cause originating a series of events that, without break in their continuity, result in accomplishment of the prime objective of employment of the broker who is producing a purchaser who is ready, willing, and able to buy real estate on the owner's terms.

Both the six factors and the recommended questions can be found in the current edition of NAR's Code of Ethics. With the hope that the problem of the procuring cause guidelines had been solved, the problem of requirements to arbitrate remained. The 1996 Working Group report also addressed this sticky area. The result was Standard of Practice 17–4, which clarifies in detail the obligations to arbitrate in specific noncontractual disputes.

NAR's Professional Standards Committee has developed policies that specifically address noncontractual commission disputes between REALTORS® associated with different firms; these disputes require arbitration rather than litigation.

The following real-life scenarios are examples of situations that are addressed by NAR's Standard of Practice 17-4:

- A listing broker has compensated a cooperative broker and another cooperative broker claims to be the "Procuring Cause."
- A buyer agent or tenant representative is compensated by the seller or landlord and not by the listing broker, and the listing broker reduces the commission owed by the seller or landlord. Subsequently another co-op broker claims "procuring cause."
- A buyer agent or tenant representative is compensated by the buyer or tenant and a second co-op broker claims "procuring cause."
- Two or more listing brokers claim entitlement to commission pursuant to open listings.

All of these situations are to be accommodated through the standard arbitration procedures and current procuring cause guidelines provided by the REALTOR® organizations. It is important for buyer agents to be very careful about interfering with another agent's client, specifically the seller—the listing agent's client. It is also important to insure that the agent not put any consumer buyer or seller in a position to have to pay a double commission.

SUMMARY

It is hoped that the current NAR procuring cause guidelines and changes in the Code of Ethics will solve many of the problems that were generated with the advent of buyer agency. It is important for buyers' agents to be very careful about interfering with another agent's client, specifically the seller, the listing agent's client. It is also important to ensure that the agent not put any consumer buyer or seller in a position to have to pay a double commission.

REVIEW QUESTIONS

1. The threshold rule, or first showing of the property, as entitlement to a commission
   a. was eliminated as the primary consideration of procuring cause in the 1990s.
   b. is still the basis used to determine procuring cause.
   c. applies only to listing agents.

ANSWER:

a. Although the threshold rule used to be the determining factor in procuring cause, who showed the property in question is only one of numerous factors looked at by today's hearing panels. Because there are many factors, the threshold rule was eliminated as the primary consideration during the 1990s. The factors apply to all agents.

2. Estrangement occurs when
   a. the broker's conduct causes the client to terminate the relationship.
   b. the buyer client lives out of town.
   c. the broker takes a vacation.

ANSWER:

a. Estrangement is similar to abandonment but results when the buyer actually terminates his or her relationship with the buyer's agent because of the agent's conduct. The fact that the buyer lives out of town is no excuse for abandonment by the agent. Likewise, unless the vacation is very long and/or the agent has made no provision for another agent to "cover," taking a vacation cannot be cause for estrangement.

CHAPTER 13

The Future of Real Estate Brokerage Relationships

Trends in agency issues are perhaps easier to predict than the mix of large, medium-sized, and small companies, as well as its division into franchises and independents. Changes in agency depend on court decisions, legislation and regulation, actions of the National Association of REALTORS®, and consumer pressures. With the exception of consumer pressures, all of these forces can be defined and their directions clearly tracked. In this final chapter, each of these forces will be analyzed, the apparent directions compared, and resulting predictions made.

COURT DECISIONS

Until the late 1960s, buyers were, more or less, on their own, as courts generally used the rule of *caveat emptor*, or buyer beware. It was up to buyers to do any investigation they felt necessary; neither agents nor sellers were under any obligation to disclose. Through the mid-1970s, this rather callous doctrine was modified to a requirement that agents had a duty to act honestly and aboveboard: misrepresentation and fraud were clearly illegal. By the late 1970s, these theories had evolved to impose a duty to act competently, holding agents to a theoretical standard of care. Since about 1983, court decisions have increasingly judged real estate licensees to be the *agents* of their principals, thus owing fiduciary duties to their client.

Courts have therefore characterized the real estate licensee not as a broker, who simply brings together willing and able buyers and sellers, but as an agent, who owes strict fiduciary duties to his or her principal, the client. This is a significant change, a change that has now reached the awareness level in the collective consciousness of the real estate industry. With this awareness comes self-questioning: If we are agents, who is it that we represent?

During the last half of the 1980s, a small minority of agents began to answer "Buyers!" The vast majority hung on to business as usual and answered "Sellers!" During the 1990s, the answers increasingly result in representation for every buyer and every seller, including dual agency for in-house transactions (except in states that provide designated brokerage and/or nonagency, where some licensees choose to switch from agency to designated brokerage and/or nonagency for in-house transactions).

LEGISLATION AND REGULATIONS

As real estate transactions have increased in complexity, legislators and/or regulators increasingly required that real estate licensees disclose their agency relationship to the public with whom they work. This movement began in the early 1980s; it picked up considerable steam during the late 1980s, and by the millennium, virtually all states had some sort of disclosure requirement.

Initially, disclosure was designed to protect buyers, as it became apparent that most buyers thought they were being represented by agents even though these agents legally represented sellers. Efforts to help all parties understand whom, if anyone, they could rely on for advice and advocacy, led to the passage of laws and regulations requiring agents to tell buyers that the agents represented the sellers as clients. They could, however, provide necessary services to buyers, not the least of which was the requirement for fair and honest information.

In the late 1980s, selling agents increasingly used this requirement of disclosure to introduce an offer of buyer representation. Although tradition and MLS rules and regulations still made them sellers' agents or subagents, they worked far more closely with buyers and eagerly accepted the legal role of buyer agency to fit the reality of practice to legal theory.

Contemporary disclosure usually requires a description of all forms of agency (and nonagency in some states). The agent then tells the consumer which of these types of agency/ nonagency are available by company policy and at this point the consumer may chose.

ACTIONS OF THE NATIONAL ASSOCIATION OF REALTORS®

As might well be expected of such a huge organization, the National Association of REALTORS® has long been a stalwart defender of the *status quo* and of the doctrine of sub-agency. Momentum favoring change began during the middle and late 1980s, as NAR leaders became increasingly aware of the legal changes that were occurring outside the association and the resulting need to make internal modifications that reflected these changes. The battles for change were hard fought, both in private and in public on the floor of the NAR board of directors.

However, change was inevitable, and during the 1990s, NAR began taking the lead rather than simply following the courts, legislators, and regulators. The organization continues to modify its Code of Ethics, Standards of Practice, and Model MLS Rules and Regulations. These modifications now acknowledge and support all forms of agency, nonagency, and designated brokerage. Major revisions for the Code of Ethics recognize the different brokerage relationships and responsibilities.

NAR, through its Legal Research Center, Inc., provides an Agency Annual Report Grid that quotes agency-related statutes and regulations state by state. These are in sufficient detail as to be useful for practical guidance for licensees in each state. For each state, the report grid lists, with relevant citations: general agency relationship requirements, relationship with buyers, relationship with sellers, transaction brokers (nonagents), dual agents, designated agents, term of relationship, general applicability of provisions, other relevant provisions, and definitions.

CONSUMER PRESSURES

During the 1980s, consumers gradually became aware that in most real estate transactions, the buyer was not represented.

As a result of media attention, many purchasers even began to search for agents who both could and would represent them. Because of media attention to the subject and the ultimate fairness of representation for both buyer and seller, definite consumer pressure exists for both buyer and seller agency. This pressure continued to increase the practice of buyer agency, in particular during the 1990s.

As mentioned in an earlier chapter, the Consumer Federation of America (CFA) joined forces with the American Association of Retired Persons (AARP) to produce a booklet for members defining the agency services available from the real estate industry. This pamphlet strongly recommended buyer agency. In January 1993, the CFA formed a coalition with NAR and ARELLO, the purpose of which was to obtain agency disclosure regulation and/or legislation in all 50 states. The characteristics of such disclosure are: timely (at first significant contact), meaningful (all possible forms of agency are disclosed), and written. This effort has been successful.

PREDICTIONS FOR THE FUTURE

The momentum of each of the forces described is in the same direction, a direction that will result in at least nine predictable results.

1. *The practice of buyer agency is becoming standard operating procedure nationwide.* When given the choice, both buyers and agents tend to elect buyer agency. As is often characteristic of trends in real estate, buyer agency has been essentially 100 percent in California since the

early 1990s. During the mid-1990s, a similar level was reached by many western states such as Utah. Percentages in the Midwest, East, and South have also increased substantially, but few approach 100 percent, as some subagency is still practiced.

2. *Single agency will become more prevalent than dual agency.* Although dual agency is legal in all but four states (Colorado, Florida, Kansas, and Vermont) with disclosure and informed consent, both agents and clients prefer the simplicity and comfort of a single-agency relationship. Knowing exactly where your allegiance and duty lie is far easier than attempting the delicate balance of dual agency, in which both parties must be represented equally in a way that is satisfactory to both.

   Dual agency is used only for in-house sales, in which a buyer client purchases a seller client's listing. Today the possibility and terms of such dual agency are disclosed to the seller at the time an agent takes a listing and to the buyer at the time he or she agrees to be a client. For salespeople who practice dual agency, the biggest challenge is keeping price and motivation confidential on both sides of the transaction so that neither buyers nor sellers lose their bargaining position.

   However, nondisclosure or improper handling of dual agency can result in substantial legal liability. In *Columbus v. Mehner,* a 2002 Alaska case, the settlement was $200,000 as a result of licensee Mehner not properly disclosing a dual agency relationship.

   Details of this practice and its documentation can be found in *Consensual Dual Agency: A Practical Approach to the In-House Sale,* by Harlan, Lyons, and well-known agency attorney and trainer John Reilly. For information, contact the authors at (800) 285-0063, fax (866) 891-4769, or at 2541 Spruce Street, Boulder, CO 80302. Information is also available via e-mail at *Gail@BoulderRealEstate.com* or *Don@Harlan-Lyons.com*.

3. *Designated agency/brokerage will be the method of choice for in-house transactions.* As of 2004, 47 percent of all states had specific provisions concerning designated agents. An additional 14 percent had statutes or regulations that effectively defined and regulated a designated agent's role without expressly providing for such an agency. For instance, in New Hampshire, regulations allow that a licensee acting "in the capacity of a non-agent" must disclose that position. Thirty-nine percent of jurisdictions surveyed by the NAR had no designated agency rules.

4. *Nonagency will become a standard option for real estate transactions with the amount of usage varying widely from state to state.* States are increasingly (32 percent in 2004) providing specific rules defining nonagency duties and responsibilities. Other states (14 percent) simply have provisions that, although they do not specifically address nonagency, implicitly regulate activities undertaken by such brokers. For example, South Carolina provides an agency exception for ministerial acts (such as writing or conveying offers) in a real estate transaction.

5. *Buyers will be listed in the MLS.* Many MLS sites and catalogs contain a section that describes the specific needs and wants of specific buyers represented by buyers' agents. Computer driven MLSs will increasingly assist

agents in matching properties and buyers, thus stream-lining the marketing and purchasing process.

6. *The relationship between sellers' agents and buyers' agents has generally become cooperative rather than defensive.* With experience and time, sellers' agents and buyers' agents have gained respect for each other's role, because to be effective, a transaction requires a buyer and a seller who agree on price and terms. During negotiations, sometimes the buyer is stronger and sometimes the seller is, but, whenever a transaction closes, there is agreement. This situation is unlike the adversarial relationship between plaintiff and defendant. Agreement between clients requires cooperation between the agents as they work to bring a contract to closing.

7. *Subagency will disappear entirely, if it has not already done so, due largely to market pressures.* It has become apparent that the increase in buyer agency has substantially reduced subagency. However, subagency also decreased when sellers become aware of their liability for the words and actions of subagents, most of whom they do not know and cannot control. There are some states, such as Colorado, that have outlawed subagency by statute.

8. *There will be an increasing unbundling of the services available from real estate licensees.* Rather than contracting for a listing agent or a buyer's agent and paying a percentage of the sales price for the agent's services, buyers and sellers will be able to choose from a menu of services that they need and for which they are willing to pay. Some services will cost a flat fee, while others will be billed on an hourly fee basis or even a percentage of the final sales price.

9. *Limited service brokerage operations in which licensees do little more than post listings in the MLS for a fee will continue to flourish although they will only represent a relatively small portion of the market.* For buyers' agents, such listings often require picking their way through a rocky ethical and legal terrain as they try to get deals closed, with little industry guidance available. The nature of the challenge in working with limited-service brokerages varies widely. For example, in Texas, buyers' agents are not permitted to communicate offers to sellers, even with permission from the listing agent.

SUMMARY

The character of real estate practice during the first part of the 21st century will be influenced by several forces: court decisions, legislation and regulation, actions of the National Association of REALTORS®, and consumer pressures. Each of these forces has pushed the industry in the direction of buyer agency, single agency rather than dual agency, increasing designated brokerage, cooperation between buyers' and sellers' agents, and the total disappearance of subagency. In addition, it is predicted that buyers will increasingly be listed on the MLS; an unbundling of services provided by real estate licensees will become a standard option with limited service brokerage as one of those options.

REVIEW QUESTIONS

1. What pressures caused buyer agency to become wide-spread?
   a. Court decisions
   b. Increases in disclosure regulations
   c. Consumer awareness
   d. All of the above

ANSWER:

d. Buyer agency has become almost universally practiced due to many factors/events occurring at the same time. These include court decisions, disclosure requirements, and consumer awareness due to such groups as the Consumer Federation of America.

2. Which of the following organizations has played a leading role in legalizing buyer agency?
   a. AFL/CIO
   b. ARELLO
   c. AAA
   d. AARP

ANSWER:

b. ARELLO is the Association of Real Estate License Law Officials; it is an association of real estate commissions and other regulators of real estate practitioners. ARELLO has been very active in providing regulations that have led to the legalization of buyers' agents.

3. Designated agency/brokerage
   a. is regulated in nearly half of the 50 states.
   b. creates an illegal relationship for buyers' agents.
   c. is used for MLS transactions (i.e., non in-house transactions).

ANSWER:

a. As of 2004, 47 percent of all states had specific provisions concerning designated agents; an additional 14 percent had statutes or regulations that effectively defined and regulated a designated agent's role without expressly providing for such an agency. Designated agency is a legal relationship that allows one agent in a company to represent the buyer while another represents the seller without creating a dual agency. Designated agency applies only to in-house transactions.

4. Fee-for-service/unbundling of services
   a. will never substitute for commissions.
   b. allows clients to pay only for the services they want.
   c. was created by the National Association of REALTORS®.
   d. is determined by agents and would not be in a company agency policy.

ANSWER:

b. Fee-for-service, that is the unbundling of real estate services such that each service has a separate fee, is one of the newest trends in the industry. Although it will probably never totally substitute for commissions, many agents and consumers are beginning to use/request such unbundling. The primary promoter and advocate of unbundling is Julie Garton-Good who is also the founder of the National Association of

Real Estate Consultants and its designation, Consumer Certified Real Estate Consultant. To offer unbundled services requires a supportive company agency policy as well as agent agreement.

Glossary

accounting The fiduciary duty requiring that the agent account for any of the principal's funds, documents, or other things of value that have been entrusted to him or her.

agency The relationship resulting from mutual consent between the principal and his or her agent that the agent will act on the principal's behalf and subject to his or her control.

agent A licensee who has agreed to act on behalf of his or her principal and subject to that principal's control.

ARELLO (Association of Real Estate License Law Officials) An international organization in which the members are regulators of real estate licensees (e.g., real estate commissioners).

blanket unilateral offer of subagency An offer that may be made by a listing agent to all other members of the MLS when he or she submits his or her seller's listing to a traditional MLS; the offer is accepted whenever an agent shows the listed property without rejecting the offer.

buyer agency The agency relationship that exists between a buyer principal and his or her buyer's agent.

buyer presentation book A professional tool that presents the broker's qualifications, experience, and education and that contains information about the buying process; this is shown to the buyer during the buyer counseling session.

buyer's kit A collection of legal documents, information on financing and the community, and sample forms, which is given to the buyer during the buyer counseling session.

client A buyer or seller who is represented by an agent who is subject to that buyer's or seller's control; also called a *principal.*

confidentiality The fiduciary duty that requires the agent to keep secret any information that his or her principal considers to be private.

conflict of interest The situation in which an agent's interests may be adverse to those of his or her principal; immediate disclosure is required.

contingent fee Any fee that is conditional upon the occurrence of some event, usually a closing.

customer Usually a buyer who is working with an agent who represents the seller; also the seller of an unlisted property that is being sold to a buyer represented by a buyer's agent; also, another broker's listed seller whose property is being purchased by your buyer client.

debt ratio The ratio of gross monthly income to monthly long-term debt; used to determine financial qualifications of a buyer.

disclosure The fiduciary duty that requires an agent to tell his or her principal all facts and information that might affect the principal's decisions concerning either the property or the transaction.

escrow An agreement whereby a third party keeps something of value for delivery on the fulfillment of some condition.

farming Activities designed to establish a long-term relationship with a group of people such that they learn to depend on a particular licensee for real estate services; can be either geographic or social in character.

FTC (Federal Trade Commission) An agency of the federal government that oversees all aspects of trade, including relationships between real estate licensees and the public.

fiduciary duty The duties of loyalty, disclosure, confidentiality, obedience, reasonable care and diligence, and accounting for all funds and documents under the agent's control that are required by common law of any agent relative to his or her principal.

flat (fixed) fee Any fee the amount of which is fixed and therefore not dependent on price; often used by buyers' agents to avoid conflict of interest.

FSBO (For Sale by Owner) Any property that is offered for sale directly by the owner and is not listed with any licensee.

hourly fee A noncontingent fee in which the agent is paid for his or her time.

housing expense ratio The ratio of total monthly housing cost (usually PITI) to gross monthly income; used to financially qualify buyers.

implied agency Any agency relationship that is indicated by the words and/or actions of the agent rather than by written agreement; also called *accidental* or *undisclosed agency*.

informed consent Any consent in which the party (buyer or seller) clearly understands what he or she is signing and why; it is obtained when the agent makes his or her explanation commensurate with the education and understanding of the party and confirms that the party does understand.

listing agent An agent of the seller who markets the seller's property, usually in the MLS, and represents the seller during the sale and closing of his or her property.

LTV (loan to value) The ratio of the loan principal amount to the property's value.

loyalty The fiduciary duty that requires the unswerving allegiance and faithfulness of the agent to his or her principal.

MLS (Multiple-Listing Service) An organized system by which members share information about listed properties; usually a committee of a board or a corporation owned by a board of REALTORS®; listed property may include a blanket unilateral offer of subagency and/or an offer of cooperation and compensation to buyers' agents.

MLS Plus An MLS policy that allowed listing agents to indicate the fee they would pay to a buyer's agent as well as the fee they would pay to a subagent upon a successful closing. Also known as *alternative MLS*. Now replaced by subagency optional and related changes to the NAR Code of Ethics.

NAR (National Association of REALTORS®) An organization of licensees in which all members swear to uphold the REALTORS®, Code of Ethics; NAR also provides education and legislative cooperation for the benefit of its members.

noncontingent fee Any fee that is not conditional on the accomplishment of an event, usually a closing.

obedience The fiduciary duty that requires an agent to obey his or her principal and fulfill the requests of his or her client to the best of his or her ability.

REALTOR® The trademarked title of any member of NAR.

reasonable care and diligence The fiduciary duty that requires that any agent provide services to his or her client that at least meet the standard of care of the industry.

retainer fee A noncontingent fee usually paid at the beginning of the agency relationship to assure the principal that the agent will work for him or her.

selling agent Any agent who sells a property; he or she may be a subagent or listing agent of the seller, a buyer's agent, a dual agent, or a nonagent. Also called a co-op agent, except when the listing agent is also the selling agent.

subagency optional MLS An MLS in which listing agents do not automatically offer subagency; the offer of cooperation and compensation may be to buyers' agents, subagents, listing agents, and/or nonagents; subagency may be offered. As of July 1, 1993, all REALTOR®-owned MLSs became subagency optional.

subagent A selling agent who has accepted a listing agent's blanket unilateral offer of subagency and is, therefore, an agent of the seller who is working with a buyer as a customer.

success fee A contingent fee that is paid only on the successful completion of the task, usually a closing; the fee may be flat or a percentage.

undisclosed dual agency A dual agency relationship that occurs when a listing agent or subagent acts and speaks as though he or she also represents the buyer but without either written or oral disclosure; see *implied agency.*

Web Site Resources

ARELLO (Association of Real Estate License Law Officials): This site gives you access to a myriad of information regarding regulation and data on both a national and state level (Canada and several other countries as well).

www.arello.org

ASHI (American Society of Home Inspectors): Site offers home inspection information for buyers, sellers, agents, and inspectors. Includes a consumer guide to home inspections that can be linked to your Web site.

www.ashi.com

CIA Fact Book: This is the site for the CIA's Fact Book, a marvelous compilation about almost every country in the world. Updated on an annual basis, it contains some of the most accurate information available.

www.odci.gov/cia/publications/factbook/geos/ xx.html

Currency Converter: Free currency converter.

www.xe.com/ucc

Census Bureau (United States): This site makes national census data available by state and neighborhood.

www.census.gov

EPA (Environmental Protection Agency): Environmental Protection Agency site. Provides information about radon gas, mold, lead-based paint, and more.

www.epa.gov

> EPA's lead-based paint information.
> *www.epa.gov/lead*

> EPA's radon information.
> *www.epa.gov/radon*

Fair Housing: Web site provides legal information, updates, and news about fair housing.

www.fairhousing.com

FTC (Federal Trade Commission) Credit Scoring: Description of credit scoring by the Federal Trade Commission.

www.ftc.gov/bcp/conline/pubs/credit/scoring.htm

Google.com Translator: Free translator (pretty good) of most foreign language texts.

www.google.com/translate

HUD (U.S. Department of Housing and Urban Development): Department of Housing and Urban Development site. You name it, if it involves housing, you'll probably find it here.

www.hud.gov

IRED (International Real Estate Digest): Site offers excellent source of current information affecting real estate worldwide.

www.ired.com

MortgageBot: Searches several mortgage sites looking for the lowest rates; contains a rate watch, ability to apply online, check loan status, and access a resource center.

www.MortgageBot.com

MSN House and Home: Microsoft's very complete site educates visitors in all aspects of the homebuying process including financing, neighborhoods, listings of homes both for sale and rent, finding an agent, making an offer, and closing. Resources and services also include furnishings, home improvements, and the MSN marketplace.

www.HomeAdvisor.com

NAEBA (National Association of Exclusive Buyer Agents): National Association of Exclusive Buyer Agents site. Provides homebuyer information, list of members, and assistance. Includes a great list of questions many buyers ask.

www.naeba.org

NAHB (National Association of Home Builders): National Association of Home Builders site. Lots of data you'd expect about home builders plus valuable resources not available anywhere else.

www.NAHB.com

Privacy Rights Clearinghouse: Detailed and excellent explanation of CLUE and A-PLUS reports including information on how to obtain them.

www.privacyrights.org/fs/fs26-CLUE.htm

Quicken Loans: Provides current rates, allows visitors to calculate answers to several important questions including home affordability, payment calculator, rent versus buy, refinance calculator, rate versus points, and credit assessment. Quick and easy to use.

www.QuickenLoans.com

Realtor.com (National Association of REALTORS®): Search your marketplace the way your buyers do. A national network of property, broker, and lender information obtained from almost all MLSs in the United States. Easy to search geographically.

www.realtor.com

Realtor.org (National Association of REALTORS®): By typing in a topic, searches back issues of *REALTOR® Magazine*, access NAR databases by division, and much more. Let NAR's 1 million+ power work for you. Check out their "Field Guide to Buyer Brokerage" (and many other relevant topics), which gives you quick access to information on the basics, FAQs, legal issues, and books and other resources.

www.realtor.org

To access the Information Central Library (National Association of REALTORS®), call (800) 874-6500. Ask for the library then let a NAR librarian search the largest real estate library in the world for the information you need. Loans of books for $10 shipping and handling.

REBAC (Real Estate Buyer's Agent Council): NAR's Real Estate Buyer's Agent Council site. Provides information about ABR designation and courses plus many, many resources for both buyers and buyers' agents.

www.rebac.net

WorldProperties.com: International Consortium of Real Estate Associations site. Provides access to member association sites (26 in 2004) including membership directories, listings, business standards, etc.

www.worldproperties.com

Appendix

Company Agency Policies

1. Seller agency exclusively whether listing or selling

_____ and its agents shall act as agents of the seller and will not act as buyer's agents. When working with buyers, _____ and its agents shall treat said buyers as customers and owe all fiduciary duties to the seller. Sellers are always clients; buyers are always customers.

As the listing agent, _____ will cooperate and split commissions with a selling agent from any other brokerage company whether said company acts as a buyer's agent, a nonagent or _____ provided such company is a member of the MLS who brings a contract acceptable to the seller.

Implementation

When securing a listing, inform the seller of our policy to represent the seller exclusively, that should the contract be presented by a _____ agent, that agent is working with the buyer as a customer only, as all _____ agents represent the seller exclusively.

Advise the seller of our policy to place listings in the MLS, thereby extending an offer of compensation to other offices that participate in the MLS. Obtain the seller's consent.

Advise the seller that agents from some brokerage companies may represent either the buyer exclusively are acting as non-agents. Explain that _____ will share our commission with such buyer agents or nonagents in exchange for their bringing in a contract acceptable to the seller and for lessening the liability of both the seller and _____.

When working with a buyer, inform the buyer as soon as possible that you and all other _____ agents represent sellers exclusively. This must be done prior to showing any property. Explain the services that _____ can offer to buyer customers and that _____ has an absolute duty to provide buyer customers with fair and honest information. Tell buyers that should they so desire they can obtain client-level representation from a lawyer or another broker and that you can refer them. Obtain the buyer's written consent.

2. Buyer agency exclusively

_____ and its agents shall act solely as buyer agents. As such, _____ and its agents shall accept no listings from sellers. Buyers are always clients; sellers are always treated as customers.

As the selling agent, _____ will seek first its compensation from the transaction with full disclosure and consent obtained from the seller and any listing agent. Should it be impossible to obtain all or part of its compensation from the transaction, the buyer will pay all or any remaining part.

Implementation

Before showing any properties, schedule a counseling interview with the buyer, during which the buyer's handbook is presented, probable transaction events are described, buyer's wants and needs are determined, an estimate of buyer's financial qualifications is made, and buyer is advised of the agency relationship and responsibilities. Obtain the buyer's signature on the buyer agency agreement.

Upon being approached by any seller, inform him or her that _____ represents buyers exclusively and therefore never takes a listing. Refer any seller to a reliable company that does take listings.

3. Single agency whether listing or selling

_____ and its agents shall act only as single agents whether representing the buyer or seller. Under no circumstances shall _____ or its agents act as dual agents.

a. As the listing agent, _____ will cooperate and split commissions with buyer's agents and nonagents. It is understood that buyer's agents relieve _____ and its sellers of liability for the words and actions of the selling agent.

b. As the selling agent, _____ will represent the buyer exclusively and will seek compensation first from the transaction according to terms agreed to in the buyer agency agreement. Only if compensation is not available from the transaction in whole or in part will _____ look to the buyer for payment.

Implementation

When working with buyers, the agent will disclose that _____ represents both buyers and sellers but never both in the same transaction. Because _____ is also a listing company, it and its agents want to avoid any possibility of dual agency by first showing the buyer any company listings that potentially meet the buyer's needs. Should the buyer decide to purchase a company listing, the buyer, at his/her sole option, will choose to either be (1) a customer and purchase through _____, or (2) referred to another company or attorney. Should no company listing satisfy the buyer, the agent shall conduct a complete counseling interview with the buyer and establish a buyer agency relationship via a signed buyer agency agreement.

To prevent the possibility of dual agency following the establishment of a buyer agency relationship, the agent shall fully communicate his buyer's needs to the Broker and any other _____ agents. If, after such buyer agency relationship is established, an owner of a property approximating the buyer's needs approaches _____ to list his or her property, such property will first be shown to the buyer client as a for-sale-by-owner and only be listed if the buyer client declines to purchase said property. Should a _____ agent show a for-sale-by-owner property, the agent shall first disclose to the seller that the agent represents the buyer and that the seller can, if he chooses, be represented by either an attorney or another real estate broker or both.

When working with a seller to secure a listing, inform the seller that our policy is to represent both sellers and buyers exclusively but never in the same transaction. In a manner similar to that described above for working with buyers, explain the procedures used to avoid dual agency and obtain the seller's consent.

Further advise the seller of our policy to place listings in the MLS, thereby extending an offer of Compensation to buyer's agents and nonagents affiliated with other companies. Obtain the seller's consent.

4. Dual agency* for in-house sales and single agency (either buyer or seller) otherwise

_____ and its agents shall act as single agents when representing either the buyer or the seller or as dual agents when selling a company listing to a buyer client. Buyers are always clients; sellers are clients only with company listings but in co-op transactions sellers are treated as customers.

*   In states that allow designated brokerage, policy #4 can easily be modified to accommodate state law.

(This policy is identical to number 3 above except that no attempt is made to avoid dual agency. Instead, when listing a buyer or a seller, disclosure is made that the company policy is one of disclosed dual agency should a buyer client decide to purchase a seller client's listing. It is explained that in the case of dual agency, _____ and its agents will not disclose to the buyer the lowest price that the seller will take nor disclose to the seller the highest price that the buyer will pay. Should there be other terms that either party considers as strictly confidential, specifics regarding these terms can be included in the dual agency amendment and thereby held as secret from the other client. Dual agency amendments are attached to both the listing contract and the buyer agency agreement; at the time of signing a purchase contract, a separate dual agency agreement is attached and the seller's and buyer's signatures are obtained, thus indicating their consent to the terms of the dual agency.)

A special, limited version of policy #4 is the following:

_____ and its agents shall preferentially act as agents of the seller and, as such, will usually treat buyers as customers. However, should the buyer fall into any of the categories listed below, _____ and its agents shall act as the buyer's agent. Further, should such a buyer client purchase a company listing, _____ and its agents shall be dual agents representing both the seller and the buyer. Thus, either seller or buyer may be either a client or a customer as determined by the policy above.

Criteria for determining buyer status:

Buyer Clients	*Buyer Customer*
Self	Any buyer not on list to the left
Buyer who wants anonymity	Open house attendee
Relative	Telephone contact
Close friend	
Business associate/partner	
Former client or customer	
First-time buyer	
Out-of-town buyer	
Buyer who wants representation	

Comments Regarding the Company Agency Policies

Policy #1 used to be the most common as it was the traditional way of doing business. Policy #2 is relatively uncommon because few brokers are willing to give up part of the real estate business, i.e., the part due to sellers' listings. Policy #4 is being elected by offices that both list properties and represent buyers. Although it openly embraces dual agency it does so only as a means of implementing buyer agency. Policy #4 is the policy of choice for a majority of offices.

It should be noted that some companies have developed policies that prohibit dual agency but allow both buyers and sellers to be represented but never in the same transaction. These policies fall into two categories: (a) the "Chinese Wall" structure and (b) the "single agency" policy. The "Chinese Wall" structure establishes two companies are established under one ownership but with separate brokers. One company only takes listings and represents sellers as clients, one company only sells properties and represents buyers as clients. The first company refers buyers to the second, the second company refers sellers to the first. The "single agency" policy (#3) provides representation for buyers and sellers but never both in the same transaction. Dual agency is avoided by establishing rigorous procedures to prevent buyer clients from purchasing seller clients' listings. Such policies are very uncommon.

In states that allow nonagency, additional policies could be added to this list. Although definitions vary from state to state, all include the inability of nonagents to be advocates for any party to the transaction. This inability removes the most important opportunities for adding value to the transaction; for this reason, nonagency practice is not expected to be a major factor in the future.

Contract Protective Clauses

Inspection

Seller agrees to provide Buyer, on or before _____, with a Seller's Property Disclosure form completed by Seller to the best of Seller's current actual knowledge. Buyer or any designee shall have the right to have inspections(s) of the physical condition of the Property and Inclusions made at Buyer's expense. If written notice of any unsatisfactory condition, signed by or on behalf of Buyer, is not received by Seller on or before _____, the physical condition of the Property and Inclusions shall be deemed to be satisfactory to Buyer. If such notice is received by Seller as set forth above, and if Buyer and Seller have not agreed, in writing, to a settlement thereof on or before _____ (Resolution Deadline), this contract shall terminate three calendar days following the Resolution Deadline; unless, within three calendar days, Seller receives written notice from Buyer waiving objection to any unsatisfactory condition.

C.L.U.E and A-Plus Reports

a. REPORTS: On or before _____, 20___, the Seller shall obtain at Seller's cost and will provide to Buyer an original "C.L.U.E." and an unaltered original "A-Plus" report accurately and fully depicting the last five (5) years of insurance claims or casualty history on the Property and,

b. REPORT CONTENTS: It is agreed that contents of these reports and the incident and nature of prior claims or casualties shall be **material** to the transaction, will be treated the same as an additional inspection item allowed to Buyer and as a Seller's Disclosure in the Seller's Property Disclosure and

c. INSPECTION PERIOD: All inspection periods shall not terminate until ten (10) calendar days after Buyer actually receives possession of the foregoing reports from the Seller.

Radon Test

The inspection of the Property shall include a radon gas test indicating a level not to exceed _____ pCi/L. Said radon gas test of the Property shall be obtained on or before _____. In the event test results show a level higher than _____ pCi/L, Seller shall, at his/her sole expense and prior to closing, have the Property mitigated and shall provide Buyer with test results indicating a level equal to or less than _____ pCi/L.

Condition and Damage to Property

Except as otherwise provided in this contract, the Property and inclusions shall be delivered in the condition existing as of the date of this contract, ordinary wear and tear excepted. In the event the Property shall be damaged by fire or other casualty prior to time of closing, in an amount of not more than ten percent (10%) of the total purchase price, Seller shall be obligated to repair the same before the date of closing. In the event such damage is not repaired within said time or if the damages exceed such sum, this contract may be terminated at the option of Buyer. Should Buyer elect to carry out this contract despite such damage. Buyer shall be entitled to credit for all the insurance proceeds resulting from such damage to the Property and Inclusions, not exceeding, however, the total purchase price. Should any Inclusion(s) or service(s) fail or be damaged between the date of this contract and the date of closing or the date of possession, whichever shall be earlier, then Seller shall be liable for the repair or replacement of such Inclusion(s) or service(s) with a unit of similar age, size and quality, or an equivalent credit, less any insurance proceeds received by Buyer covering such repair or replacement.

Title Insurance

A "satisfactory" title document shall contain:

a. a narrow tax exception that excepts only taxes for the current year, not yet due or payable;

b. affirmative "gap" coverage that insures against loss or damage by reason of there being recorded title encumbrances that first appear in the public records subsequent to the effective date of the Commitment, but prior to the effective date of the Policy;

c. deletion of the four preprinted exceptions.

Interest on Earnest Money Deposit

The parties instruct the Broker holding earnest money to place Buyer's deposit into an interest-bearing account with all interest to be credited to Buyer at closing. Buyer will pay any processing fee required and all costs of setting up, maintaining, and closing the account. Buyer understands that such fees and costs may exceed the interest earned.

Encroachment

If the survey reveals an encroachment(s) onto an adjoining Property or onto the Property by an adjoining owner, then such encroachment either shall be removed or Seller shall obtain an agreement(s) addressing such boundary matters with the adjoining owner(s), which is contingent on Buyer's approval. If neither occurs within _____ (____) days of discovery or by the scheduled closing date, whichever occurs earlier, Buyer may accept the encroachment(s) or elect to terminate this contract.

Property Condition and Maintenance

Seller agrees that, at closing, if applicable, the air-conditioning equipment, electrical, lighting, sewer, cesspool/septic tank, drainage, lawn sprinkler system, plumbing system (including solar water heater), all major appliances, and mechanical devices (including all locks and window hardware) shall be in good mechanical repair and working order consistent with their age; otherwise Seller shall repair or replace such items prior to closing. Seller shall maintain until closing the interior and exterior of the Property, existing landscaping, grounds, lawn, and pool in the same or better condition and repair as they were on the acceptance date of this Contract. All of the foregoing shall be at Seller's sole cost and expense.

Walk Through and Appliance Check

Buyer may complete Buyer's walk-through personally or by a representative of Buyer's choice prior to the scheduled time and date of closing; otherwise this right of inspection shall be deemed waived. If any repairs and maintenance required under the Property Condition and Maintenance clause have not been made by closing, Seller agrees that an amount equal to one hundred fifty percent (150%) of the estimated cost of repair shall be held in escrow until the repairs are completed; provided, however, that any remaining funds held will be automatically disbursed to Buyer by escrow if all repairs are not completed within _____ (____) days after closing. All repair bills will be paid through escrow and any balance remaining after completion of all repairs shall be returned to Seller.

Interior and Exterior Cleaning

Prior to closing, Seller shall, at Seller's expense, have cleaned the interior of the improvements on the Property. Such cleaning shall include all appliances, floors, carpets, windows, jalousies, and screens. Seller shall also dispose of all trash, junk, and brush both within or outside any improvements located on the Property.

Pet Related Carpet Treatment

Prior to closing, Seller shall, at Seller's expense, remove any pets from the Property, have the carpets within the improvements of the Property professionally cleaned, and the interior of the Property treated for fleas/ticks by a professional.

Appraisal

Buyer shall have the right to terminate this contract if the purchase price exceeds the Property's valuation determined by an appraiser engaged by _____. If Seller receives a copy of such appraisal or written notice from lender which confirms the Property's valuation is less than the purchase price, on or before _____, this contract shall terminate. Buyer shall have the privilege and option of proceeding with consummation of this contract without regard to the amount of the appraised valuation.

Dual Agency Agreement

DUAL AGENCY ADDENDUM
(for Listing Contracts)

This Dual Agency Addendum is part of a:

❏ Buyer Agency Contract, dated _____ 20_____ ,

❏ Listing Contract, dated _____ 20_____ ,

between the broker named below and its sales agents ("Broker") and the undersigned buyer or seller ("Principal").

Buyer is interested in viewing any property which meets buyer's needs, including those which may be listed by Broker. Seller is interested in marketing seller's property to any prospective buyer, including buyers who have an agency relationship with Broker. The undersigned Principal acknowledges that:

1. A real estate broker, when acting for one principal, has duties that include undivided loyalty, confidentiality, and full disclosure, but only to *one* principal.
2. Dual agency creates a conflict of interest because the broker's duties of confidentiality, full disclosure, and loyalty to one party conflict with those same duties to the other.
3. A real estate broker can, however, be the dual agent of both seller and buyer in the same transaction, but only when seller, buyer, and the broker so consent.

Principal and Broker now agree to modify Broker's duties so that Broker may act as a dual agent. Principal consents to and waives objections to the conflict of interest created by Broker acting as a dual agent.

If Broker becomes a dual agent, and so informs the Principal, Broker agrees not to disclose to either seller or buyer, without the prior consent of the other, any of the following things:

A. Material information about the other party, unless the disclosure is required by law, or unless failure to disclose would constitute fraud or dishonest dealing.

B. That buyer will pay a price or agree to terms other than those contained in the offer, or that seller will accept a price or terms other than those contained in the listing.

C. The motivation of the buyer to buy or the seller to sell.

Broker shall disclose to the buyer all material facts about the physical condition of property actually known to Broker.

This Addendum will control in the event of any conflict with the contract to which it is attached.

Principal understands and agrees that all "comparable" property information available through the Multiple Listing Service or otherwise, including listed and sold properties, may be disclosed to both Seller and Buyer at any time and may be accompanied by a Comparative Market Analysis prepared by the respective Sales Agents of the Seller and the Buyer.

Additional provisions:

Principal (Seller/Buyer): _____ Date_____

_____ Date_____

Broker: _____

By: _____ Date_____

This is a legal instrument. If not understood, legal, tax ,
or other counsel should be consulted before signing.

DUAL AGENCY CONSENT AGREEMENT

(for Purchase Sale Contracts)

Property Address _____

Date: _____

Seller(s): _____

Buyer(s): _____

1. Seller and Buyer hereby acknowledge and agree that
   _____ (name of Company) and all of
   its agents (herein collectively called "Broker") are representing
   both Buyer and Seller in the purchase and sale of the above ref-
   erenced property and that Broker has been and is now the
   Agent of both Seller and Buyer with respect to this transaction.
   Seller and Buyer have both consented to, and *hereby confirm their
   consent to, this dual representation.*

2. Seller and Buyer:

   (A) agree that Broker shall not be required to and shall not
       disclose to either Buyer or Seller any personal, financial,
       or other confidential information to the other party
       without the express written consent of that party other
       than information related to material property defects
       which are known to Broker, adverse material facts con-
       cerning Buyer's financial ability to perform the terms of
       the transaction and whether Buyer intends to occupy
       Property as a principal residence, and other information
       Broker is required by law to disclose. Confidential infor-
       mation shall include but not be limited to any price
       Seller is willing to accept that is less than the listing price
       or any price Buyer is willing to pay that is higher than
       that offered in writing;

   (B) acknowledge notification that (i) dual agency can create
       conflict of interest for Broker; (ii) Seller and Buyer each
       forfeit their individual right to receive the undivided loy-
       alty of Broker;

(C) waive any claim now or hereafter arising out of any conflicts of interest the dual agency may cause.

3. Both Seller and Buyer agree that all "comparable" property information available through the Multiple Listing Service or otherwise, including listed and sold properties, may be disclosed to both Seller and Buyer at any time and may be accompanied by a Comparative Market Analysis prepared by the respective Sales Agents of the Seller and the Buyer.

4. Both parties understand and agree that Broker shall have the right to collect a commission or fee from the Seller or from the Buyer or both, and acknowledge that it has been disclosed that in connection with this transaction, Broker will collect a total fee of $_____ or _____% of the sales price; said fee shall be shown as a debit to the Seller and thus included in the sales price paid by the Buyer.

5. **Both parties are advised to seek competent legal and tax advice with regard to this transaction, and with regard to all documents executed in connection with this transaction, including this Dual Agency Consent Agreement.**

6. Seller and Buyer recognize and agree that this document does not replace those documents signed earlier, i.e. the Exclusive Buyer Agency Agreement signed by the Buyer on _____, 20_____, and the Exclusive Right to Sell Listing Agreement signed by the Seller on _____, 20_____. However, in any areas where this document contradicts or conflicts with those documents, this Dual Agency Consent Agreement shall supersede. This agreement hereby becomes a part of the attached Purchase and Sale Contract.

I HAVE READ AND UNDERSTAND THE ABOVE AGREEMENT.

Buyer(s): _____
                                                                    date

Seller(s): _____
                                                                    date

Exclusive Buyer
Agency Contract

Exclusive Buyer Agency Contract

_____

(Place)

_____

(Date)

_____

(Buyer(s))
(hereinafter referred to as ("Buyer") hereby appoints _____

_____

(Broker's Name and Address)
(hereinafter referred to as "Broker") as Buyer's exclusive agent for the purposes set forth in Section 2 hereof and under the terms specified herein.

Section 1. _Effect of Exclusive Buyer Agency Contract._ By appointing Broker as Buyer's exclusive agent, Buyer agrees to conduct all negotiations for property of the type described in Section 2 hereof through Broker, and to refer to Broker all inquiries received in any form from real estate brokers, salespersons, prospective sellers, or any other source, during the time this agency contract is in effect. In addition, Buyer agrees that any Broker compensation which is conditioned upon the acquisition by Buyer of interests in real property whether by lease or purchase will be earned by Broker whenever such interests in real property are acquired by Buyer, or by Buyer through any person or entity, without any discount or allowance for any efforts made by Buyer or by any other agent of Buyer in connection with the acquisition of such interests in real property.

Section 2. *Purpose(s) of Agency.* Buyer desires to purchase or lease real property (which may include items of personal property) described as follows:

Type: ( )Residential   ( )Residential Income ( )Other

          ( )Commercial ( )Industrial   ( )Vacant Land

General Description: _____

_____

_____

Approximate Price Range: $_____to $_____

General Location: _____

_____

_____

Section 3. *Time of Commencement and Duration of Agency.* Broker's authority   as   Buyer's   exclusive   agent   shall   begin _____, 20_____, and shall continue until _____, 20_____, unless sooner terminated by written notice of termination given by one party to the other, or by completion of the purpose(s) of agency as set forth in Section 2 hereof, subject to the following subsections:

(a) *Termination by Buyer.* Subject to the provisions of Section 6(c), in the event of termination by Buyer prior to completion of the purpose(s) of agency, and prior to the termination date set forth in this Section 3, by written notice of termination given to Broker by Buyer, Broker shall be reimbursed by Buyer for all expenditures reasonably incurred by Broker pursuant to this agency contract. (b) *Termination by Broker.* In the event of termination by Broker prior to the completion of the purpose(s) of agency, and prior to the termination date set forth in this Section 3, by written notice of termination given to

Buyer by Broker, Buyer shall be under no obligation to Broker, except for obligations existing at the time of termination or arising out of Section 6 hereof, and Buyer shall have no claim against Broker arising out of this agency contract, except for any claim founded upon Broker's negligence or Broker's breach of fiduciary duty.

Section 4. *Broker's Representations and Services.* Broker represents that Broker is duly licensed under the laws of the State of _____ as a real estate broker, and agrees that Broker will use Broker's best efforts as Buyer's agent to locate property as described in Section 2 hereof and to procure acceptance of any offer to purchase or lease such property. Broker shall make submissions to Buyer describing and identifying properties appearing to Broker substantially to meet the criteria set forth in Section 2, for the consideration of Buyer.

Section 5. *Costs of Services or Products Obtained from Outside Sources.* Broker will not obtain or order products or services from outside sources unless Buyer agrees in writing to pay for them immediately when payment is due. (Examples: surveys, soil tests, title reports, engineering studies)

Section 6. *Compensation of Broker.* In consideration of the services to be performed by Broker, Buyer agrees to pay Broker as follows: [Instruction: If any of the forms of compensation set forth in subsection (a), (b) or (c) will not be used, write "N/A: in the blank(s) of such subsection(s).)]

(a) *Retainer Fee.* Buyer will pay Broker a nonrefundable retainer fee of $_____ due and payable upon signing of this agency contract. (   )Fee shall be credited against success fee or (   )Fee shall be retained in addition to success fee.

(b) *Hourly Fee.* Buyer will pay Broker at the rate of $_____ per hour for the time spent by Broker pursuant to this agency contract, to be paid to Broker when billed to Buyer. (   )Fee shall be credited against success fee or (   ) Fee shall be considered full payment.

(c) *Success Fee.* Parties hereby agree that Broker shall first seek compensation from the transaction. Should the fee so obtained be greater than that listed in subsection (1) or (2) hereof, Broker shall pay Buyer the difference at closing. Should the fee so obtained be less than that listed in subsection (1) or (2) hereof, Buyer shall pay Broker the difference at closing. If fee cannot be obtained from the transaction in whole or in part, Buyer will pay Broker a fee according to either subsection (1) or subsection (2) below, as follows:

(1) If at the time Buyer contracts to buy or lease such property it is subject to an exclusive right to sell listing contract, a fee equal to the greater of $_____ or _____% of the purchase or lease price.

(2) If at the time Buyer contracts to buy or lease such property it is not subject to an exclusive right to sell listing contract, a fee equal to the greater of $_____ or _____% of the purchase or lease price. The provisions of subsections (1) and (2) above are conditioned upon successful completion of the purpose(s) of agency set forth in Section 2 hereof, or the acceptance by Buyer of a transaction not in exact compliance with the terms specified in Section 2 hereof, but within the purview of this agency contract. This fee is due and payable upon closing of the transaction(s), subject to the provisions of Section 7 hereof. This fee shall apply to transactions made during the original terms of this agency contract or made during any extension of such original or extended terms, and shall also apply to transactions made within _____ days after this agency contract expires or is terminated if the property acquired by Buyer was submitted in writing to Buyer by Broker pursuant to Section 4 hereof during the original term or any extension of the term of this agency contract.

Section 7. *Failure to Close Agreements Made Pursuant to the Agency.* If a seller or lessor in an agreement made on behalf of Buyer fails to close such agreement, with no fault on the part of Buyer, the success fee provided in Section 6, subsection (c), shall be waived. If such transaction fails to close because of any fault on the part of Buyer, such success fee will not be waived, but will be due and payable immediately. In no case shall Broker be obligated to advance funds for the benefit of Buyer in order to complete a closing.

Section 8. *Disclosure of Broker's Role.* At the time of initial contact, Broker shall inform all prospective Sellers, and their agents, with whom Broker negotiates pursuant to this agency contract, that Broker is acting on behalf of a buyer-principal, and shall be paid first from the transaction and, if such compensation is not obtainable in full or in part, by such buyer-principal.

Section 9. *Disclosure of Buyer's Identity.* (   )Broker does have Buyer's permission (   )Broker does not have Buyer's permission to disclose Buyer's identity to third parties without prior written consent of Buyer.

Section 10. *Other Potential Buyers.* Buyer understands that other potential buyers may consider, make offers on, or purchase through Broker the same or similar properties as Buyer is seeking to acquire. Buyer consents to Broker's representation of such other potential buyers before, during, and after the expiration of this Agreement.

Section 11. *Indemnification of Broker.* Buyer agrees to indemnify Broker and to hold Broker harmless on account of any and all loss or damage arising out of this agency contract, provided Broker is not at fault, including, but not limited to, attorneys' fees reasonably incurred by Broker.

Section 12. *Conflicting Interests.* If, as to any interest in real property within the scope of the purpose(s) of agency as set forth in Section 2 hereof, Broker has any ownership interest, or has any listing contract with the owner for sale or lease of the property under which he or she may be collecting a commission, and Buyer indicates interest in such property, the Broker shall immediately notify Buyer of the facts regarding Broker's interest in such real property or Broker's contractual relationship with its owner. In such event, the Buyer, at his sole option, may elect to either terminate this contract as provided in Section 3, subsection (a), or effect the terms of the dual agency agreement hereby attached.

If the purpose(s) of agency, as set forth in Section 2 hereof, include acquisition of more than one parcel of real property, the provisions of this Section 12 shall be applied only in respect to the parcel(s) as to which Broker has any of the interests or contractual relationships described in the preceding paragraph of this Section 12.

Section 13. *Assignment by Buyer.* No assignment of Buyer's right under this agency contract and no assignment of rights in real property obtained for Buyer pursuant to this agency contract shall operate to defeat any of Broker's rights under this agency contract.

Section 14. *Nondiscrimination.* The parties agree not to discriminate against any prospective seller or lessor because of the race, creed, color, sex, marital status, national origin, familial or handicapped status of such person.

Section 15. *Attorneys' Fees.* In case of litigation concerning the rights of Buyer or Broker pursuant to this agency contract, the parties agree that the Court shall award reasonable attorneys' fees to the prevailing party.

Section 16. *Modification of This Agency Contract.* No modification of any of the terms of this agency contract shall be valid, binding upon the parties or entitled to enforcement unless such modification has first been reduced to writing and signed by the parties.

Section 17. *Legal Counsel.* Broker hereby advises Buyer to seek legal, tax, and other professional advice relating to any proposed transaction. Broker does not make any representation or warranty with respect to the advisability of or the legal effect of any transaction contemplated by Buyer.

Section 18. *Entire Agreement.* This agency contract constitutes the entire agreement between the parties relating to the subject thereof, and any prior agreements pertaining thereto, whether oral or written, have been merged and integrated into this agency contract.

Section 19. *Additional Provisions.* (The following provisions may be added:

A. RE: *Section 3.* During the term of this contract, should it be determined by Buyers or Broker that continuation of this agreement is not in the best interest of either or both parties, this contract may be terminated with seven (7) days written notice.

B. RE: *Limitation on Disclosure.* Confidential information obtained by Broker in the course of any previous agency relationship with any other client will not be disclosed to Buyer. Any confidential information about Buyer learned by Broker in the course of this agency relationship will not be disclosed without Buyer's express consent or unless required by law.

C. RE: *Section 10. Other Buyers.* Should Broker represent other Buyers who are interested in the same property as Buyer, Buyer hereby agrees that Broker shall not disclose the terms of any Buyer's purchase offer to any other buyer client.

D. RE: *Section 12. Dual Agency.* Buyers understand that Broker is in the business of representing both buyers and sellers as an agent for purchases and sales of real property, and is aware that in the scope of Broker's business, Broker may obtain listing contracts for the sale of real property. Should Buyers decide to purchase property subject to an Exclusive Right to Sell Listing Contract with this Broker, Buyer hereby consents that Broker may act as a "Dual Agent" in said transaction. In the case of activation of the dual agency:

1. Broker is to disclose to Seller or prospective Seller only information authorized by Buyer for such disclosure and "material facts" which, by law, must be disclosed;

2. Broker shall make no representations to Seller on Buyer's behalf or to Buyer on Seller' behalf without permission of the representative party;

3. Broker's position as a dual agent shall be neutral with respect to both parties and Broker shall act effectively as a mediator between the parties;

4. A "Dual Agency Consent Agreement" shall be fully executed by Buyer and Sellerand made an integral part of any Purchase/Sale Contract.

E. Buyer understands that Broker shall disclose to any prospective Seller all adverse material facts actually known by Broker, including but not limited to adverse material facts concerning Buyer's financial ability to perform the terms of the transaction whether Buyer intends to occupy Property as a principal residence.

This agreement executed in multiple copies and my signature hereon acknowledges that I have received a signed copy.

Accepted_____

_____
          (Broker)   (Buyer)

By: _____

_____
                                       (Buyer)

Phone:_____

_____

                          _____
                          (Address)
                          _____
                          (Phone)

Index